sex, lies, and videotape

sex, lies, and videotape

steven soderbergh

PERENNIAL LIBRARY

HARPER & ROW, PUBLISHERS, New York
Grand Rapids, Philadelphia, St. Louis, San Francisco
London, Singapore, Sydney, Tokyo, Toronto

The author gratefully acknowledges permission to reproduce the photographs that appear on page 175 and insert 1, 2, 4–17, 19–22, copyright © 1989 Outlaw Productions. All Rights Reserved. Courtesy of Outlaw Productions and RCA/Columbia Pictures Home Video.

Credits for photographs are as follows: page 175 and insert 1, 2, 4–17, 19, 20, 22: Diana Kay Wilkins; insert 21: Walt Lloyd; pages 11 and 203: self-timer.

FIRST EDITION

Designed by Cassandra J. Pappas

Library of Congress Cataloging-in-Publication Data
Soderbergh, Steven, 1963–
  Sex, lies, and videotape / Steven Soderbergh.—1st ed.
    p. cm.
  ISBN 0-06-055202-6
  ISBN 0-06-096526-6 (pbk.)
  1. Sex, lies, and videotape. I. Title.
PN1997.S3818S63 1990
791.43′72—dc20   89-81467

90 91 92 93 94 CC/RRD 10 9 8 7 6 5 4 3 2 1
90 91 92 93 94 CC/RRD 10 9 8 7 6 5 4 3 2 1 (pbk.)

For Tar,
who waits.

introduction

You will need to know some things.

This book is in diary form, meaning there was no attempt to explain or clarify certain people or surroundings to an imaginary reader. It is my hope that this introduction, coupled with sheer repetition and implied context, will provide a sufficient foundation for understanding. When in doubt, you might try consulting the film's credit list.

I personally feel cheated whenever a reprinted screenplay has had its type reset or is not actually the real screenplay but a continuity of the finished film. I feel that the way a screenplay is written says much about the writer's sensibility, so at my request the screenplay reprinted in this book is a photostat of the actual script that stuttered out of my temperamental printer two days before shooting started, replete with typos, bad grammar, and stupid ideas that were later changed (for the better, we hoped. You be the judge).

In January 1977, my father, noting my interest in movies and realizing my talent for baseball was not sufficient to provide me with a career, enrolled me in an animation class being offered to teenagers by Louisiana State University film students. Despite my talent for drawing, animation seemed too much work for too little result, and I quickly gravitated toward grabbing the Nizo off the copystand and shooting live action. Soon I began hanging out with the college film class after school. The class was taught by Michael McCallum, and among its many talented students were Paul Ledford and Joseph

Wilkins, who became close friends in addition to being fellow film-makers.

From 1977 to 1979 I made four short films. The first was an untitled exploration of the aftereffects of Ex-Lax, starring my brother-in-law. Mainly it was an excuse to use camera angles and editing I had seen in other films. The second was entitled *October 16, 1977,* a documentary about a section of my high school that burned down. Next was *Passages,* a mood piece about dreams again starring my brother-in-law, with a guest appearance by my younger brother. Not much story here, just more practice with camera placement and editing. The fourth film of this period was *Janitor,* my first dialogue film with real actors (the others had only music and sound effects). It was an imitation of several films, mostly *Taxi Driver* and *The Conversation,* and showing this film to the class and feeling the negative reaction, I began to realize that the films I had made revealed only my interest in other films and nothing about myself. My friends' films tended to be experimental in nature but very personal, and I decided to explore this area as well.

January 1980 saw the completion of *Skoal,* a twenty-minute black-and-white experimental collage designed only to record my state of mind during my last year of high school. It was so personal that I usually didn't stay to watch the reaction. People seemed to respond to its highly personal tone, however, and it remains one of my better works.

I went to San Francisco in July 1980 to live with my sister armed with $1200 I had saved and a contact that led to the ex-wife of a well-known documentary filmmaker. Although the woman was very nice and extremely well-intentioned, she really had no way of helping me. My sister knew a guy who had worked as a production assistant on *Invasion of the Body Snatchers,* and I contacted him about work possibilities. He too was sympathetic but powerless to help. I realized that I had blown these "contacts" into something that they weren't, and to avoid depression, I began writing my first full-length script and hoped for a miracle. In September Michael McCallum called and asked if I wanted to work with him and Afshin Chamasmany (another member of the LSU film class) in Los Angeles on an NBC television show called "Games People Play" (which was cohosted by Bryant Gumbel). I said yes.

On "Games People Play" I was primarily an editor. Afshin edited as well, in addition to being head cameraman, so the three of us formed a lean, mean production team, and later we brought in Paul

Ledford to do some sound for us. During this period, Michael and I were walking to our room one night when Michael spotted a Volkswagen with an LSU decal on its window and said it looked like Brad Johnson's car. Brad had taken the very first film class at LSU and then gone to work as a production assistant for ABC through a contact Michael had given him. Strangely enough, it *was* Brad. He had just been relocated to Los Angeles by Showtime Entertainment, the new company he was working for.

By the end of 1980 I was spending almost all of my time in Los Angeles, and decided that I should move from San Francisco. By phone I contacted Larry Blake, a filmmaker and budding sound historian from New Orleans who I'd met momentarily in 1978 through Chuck Farrier, a mutual friend (Chuck taught me still photography in high school and shot *Skoal* for me). Larry was living in Los Angeles, and he spoke of a project he was to be involved with that I might be able to work on as well.

In January 1981, "Games People Play" was canceled because the actors' strike that had spawned it finally ended. I decided to move to Los Angeles anyway, hoping the project with Larry would come through. Fortunately for me, I had become close friends with Brad Johnson, and he not only provided me with a place to stay, but kept me employed with various jobs as well (re-editing shows, holding cue cards, etc.). In February I had finished the first draft of my first screenplay, entitled *After School*, which was about high school, of course. The responses were not enthusiastic. Bill Magee, a writer friend of Larry's, put it most succinctly: "Who wants to see a film about high school?" Despite Bill's comments I sublet his apartment in Hollywood, as he was leaving to move back to Charlottesville (where I had lived between 1973 and 1976. His soon-to-be wife actually knew the girl I had a crush on in eighth grade). Larry continued to wait for word on the project that would employ him, and I waited as well. Brad kept us in mind, eventually giving us jobs as scorekeepers on a game show he created for Showtime called "Laff-A-Thon" (I once made the wrong guy win. No, Brad didn't fire me). I remember Arsenio Hall being a contestant on the show.

By the fall of 1981 I was pretty discouraged. I left for Baton Rouge in October and immediately started work on another short film, which I financed by working as a still photographer for a local commercial director.

Rapid Eye Movement was completed in December 1982. It was a thirteen-minute black-and-white impression of my unsuccessful stint in Hollywood, and many of my friends insist it is still my best film. By the time it was finished, I was working in a video arcade as a coin attendant, making $70 a week and living with Joseph Wilkins, who (along with Paul Ledford) played opposite me in *Rapid Eye Movement.* After my employer at the arcade refused to pay me more than my customary two dollars an hour for my fourteen-hour Christmas Day shift, I thought I'd better look for other work. Paul had recommended me to Park Seward, the owner of Video Park, Inc., a newly formed video production company, and within months I went to work full-time for Park, again doing everything from editing to sweeping up.

In early 1983 I completed another screenplay, *Gumshoe,* an infantile comedy that Joseph rightly suggested I throw away (I was still trying to salvage *After School,* with no luck. Bill Magee was right). During my period at Video Park, I got occasional calls from Brad Johnson, who would fly me to Los Angeles to re-edit programs Showtime had purchased. In early 1984 a colleague of Brad's, Elizabeth Cantillon, recommended me to the management of the Yes group as a candidate to make an on-the-road documentary about the band's current tour. I sent off a copy of *Rapid Eye Movement* and a video I had made for a band in New Orleans, and was told I had the job. I recruited Larry as sound man and we went on the road for ten days. I returned to Video Park to cut the footage together, and feeling rebellious, edited a rather irreverent thirty-minute program. I sent the finished version off and went back to my regular work at Video Park. I was also finishing up a new screenplay, *Putting on Airs,* that I hoped to finance independently. A few weeks later, Tony Dimitriades, the Yes group's manager, called and said the group loved the documentary and wanted to know if I could fly to London and re-edit their new video. I said yes.

During my two-week assignment in Europe, Tony Dimitriades told me the group was going to make a concert film in the fall, and he wanted to know if I would act as liaison between the group and the eventual director/production company for the concert film. I said no. The day after I left London I was in Houma, Louisiana, as a tape operator on a commercial in which a guy cut up an audio speaker with a chain saw.

Tony Dimitriades phoned in August 1984 to offer me the job of directing the concert film for Yes and I said yes. I formally retired from Video Park, Inc., and worked as director and editor on the concert film until its completion in April 1985. While cutting the show in November/December '84, I rented an editing room from Wedding-ton Prods., a sound effects editing facility co-owned by a friend of Larry's, Mark Mangini. Mark and I became good friends, and I discussed with him my plans to make a low-budget feature. He offered his facility at a reduced rate when and if that happened. While Charlex was creating the extensive special effects for the show in the spring of '85, John Hardy asked me to direct a commercial for him. John co-owned one of the biggest and best ad agencies in Baton Rouge, and I had met him while I was working at Video Park. The commercial came out well, and we talked about the possibility of making an independent feature in Baton Rouge.

In the summer of 1985 I found myself in somewhat of a quandary. Although the concert film had turned out okay, I didn't see that my career as a filmmaker was going anywhere. Mary Klauser, who worked in the Yes offices, listened to my lament and suggested that I get an agent. She dialed an agent friend of hers, Ann Dollard, and four hours later I had an agent. I liked Ann very much, and she was very adept at sending me to meet people with sensibilities similar to mine. One of those people was Nick Wechsler, an executive looking to become an independent producer.

Ann thought *Putting on Airs* showed promise, but encouraged me to do more writing, so in the fall I wrote three new screenplays back-to-back: *Proof Positive, Crosstalk,* and *State of Mind. Crosstalk* eventually got me a job rewriting a television movie for Disney (which was never produced), and *State of Mind* got me a job writing an urban musical for Tri-Star called *Across the Line,* based on an idea by Mike Mahern (which was never produced). In the fall of '86 I used what Tri-Star money I hadn't spent to make another short film called *Winston.* A fourteen-minute drama (again in black-and-white), *Winston* dealt with themes not dissimilar to *sex, lies:* deception and alienation within the confines of a relationship.

The opening months of 1987 were difficult, personally and professionally. Despite being in a melancholy state after confessing some past transgressions to my ex-girlfriend, I managed to complete a new screenplay entitled *Dead From The Neck Up,* which was, of all things, a slapdash comedy. In the summer of 1987 Bob Newmyer and John Kao, owners of an independent production company called Outlaw Productions, optioned *Dead From The Neck Up,* and we worked through three more drafts and then tried unsuccessfully to get the project set up. In October I decided that I had to go back to Los Angeles and make one more concerted effort at breaking into the film business. I sold everything I owned except for my car and my books and planned to leave after Christmas. Bob Newmyer and John Kao had also hired me to write a spy thriller called *Revolver,* but as I worked on the outline, I began to be distracted by another idea for a script that I couldn't quite put my finger on. This new idea was pressing against the inside of my chest so intensely that on December 24th, four days before my scheduled departure from Baton Rouge, I sat down and started writing. This book begins at that exact moment.

Having made only one feature film, I don't feel comfortable or justified in putting forth any real filmmaking "theories." It's my *feeling* that nobody has the market cornered on good ideas, and that you should be open to suggestion and keep your eyes and ears open at all times. It's my *belief* that there should be a chain of command on a film set, but not a chain of respect (I have worked as the lowest member of a film crew and been treated like a no-class citizen by the "above-the-line" people. The experience was unpleasant but illuminating). But it's my guess that no two filmmakers work alike, which is as it should be. Personally, I like to have a good time. I mean, it's just a movie; we're not solving world hunger, right?

Someone more wise than myself said that for all the praise one receives, expect the same amount in criticism at a later date, and indeed, the most frequently asked question in the 350-odd interviews I gave this year (other than "What question are you asked the most?") was "Do you feel pressured by expectations for your second film?" The answer is no. Firstly, I'd be very disappointed if *sex, lies* were the best film I ever made. I like the film, and I think if you read this book you'll see that it's better than the script I wrote, but I can do better, and more importantly, I *should* do better. My expectations for myself must exceed the expectations of others. The alternative is mediocrity, in my opinion. Secondly, I feel somewhat blessed that there will *be* a second film, seeing as how some don't get the opportunity to make a first film, much less get the kind of release and response we were fortunate enough to get.

I have tried not to analyze why this film was successful, for fear of trying to duplicate that success in a calculated fashion in the future. I followed my instincts, and so far they have served me well. Some people don't believe (or understand) that for me the *process* of making a film is the reward. At the same time, filmmaking is a business, and if your films don't return their investment, you don't get to make films (there are exceptions, of course). I feel a compulsion to weigh the accessibility of an idea against the cost of executing it properly. To me, making an idea accessible doesn't necessarily mean dilution or compromise; it can mean clarity of execution. I think *The Metamorphosis* is a pretty obscure idea for a novel, but I think the execution is remarkably accessible.

But enough of what I think; you've got plenty of that coming. I'm happy that Harper & Row wanted to do this book, and I'm happy that my editor, Christine Schillig, let me have my way with her, in the publishing sense. I am deeply indebted to Charlotte Sheedy for letting me know of Christine's interest, and leading me through a world I still know nothing about. I offer my most sincere apology to Diana Kay Wilkins, the unpaid still photographer on *sex, lies* who took almost all the pictures for this book, and was left off the credit list of the film due to my carelessness.

For those aspiring to a career in the film business, I offer this equation: Talent + Perseverance = Luck. Be ready when it happens.

STEVEN SODERBERGH
27 NOV 89
Charlottesville, VA

item no. 7 from 1986 notebook:
    A film about deception and lost earrings.

item no. 38 from 1986 notebook:
    Everybody has a past.

item no. 48 from 1986 notebook:
    Friend on the couch. Affair with the wife.

before

Somewhere in Central Texas, 4:46 p.m., 28 DEC 87.

24 DEC 87 BATON ROUGE

Black screen. Titles. An obscene rhythmic sucking noise.

CUT TO:

DJ emptying a large can of Sweet Sue chicken dumplings into a skillet.

> DJ
>
> He made me talk to Mel Gibson.

> JC
>
> He what?

> DJ
>
> He made me talk to Mel Gibson.

> JC
>
> I don't understand. He *knows* Mel Gibson? He got him on the phone?

> DJ
>
> No, no, no. I was telling him about being self-conscious, how I've always been self-conscious about the way I look. And he said How would you like to look, what is your ideal?, and I thought for a minute, and I said Mel Gibson.

DJ *(cont.)*

So then he motions to the chair next to me and says Imagine
Mel Gibson is sitting there, what would you say to him?
Well, I felt kind of stupid, pretending that Mel Gibson was
sitting next to me.

JC

Uh-huh.

DJ

But he pushed me on it. He said Did I think I would have
anything to ask him?

JC

Who, Dr. Flick?

DJ

No, Mel Gibson, did I have anything to ask Mel Gibson, and
I thought, yeah, I would ask Mel if he was happy knowing
that lots of people found him attractive.

JC

What'd he say?

DJ

Who, Dr. Flick?

JC

No, Mel Gibson. What did he pretend to say?

DJ

He said yes.

JC

How did you feel when he said yes?

DJ

That's exactly what Dr. Flick asked me. I said I felt worse
and that I wished he had never brought Mel Gibson into
this.

JC

What did he say to that?

DJ

He said he *didn't* bring Mel Gibson into this, I did, because I picked him as my ideal.

JC

But he asked you to pick an ideal, I mean, if it wasn't Mel Gibson it would've been somebody else.

DJ

That's exactly what I told him.

JC

And what did he say?

DJ

He said I was being combative and I needed four years of therapy, minimum.

JC

(looks at dumplings)

I think those are done.

* * *

It's not right. Neither of them seem like the guy I want on the couch. They both seem too normal, not at all like someone who would intrigue/disorient Ann. Is this a comedy or a drama? Maybe JC is Ann's husband.

I just wrote the first scene between Ann and Dr. Flick, but it's too on-the-point. She's too articulate, even though she claims otherwise. I know the issue isn't really the friend on the couch, it's her marriage, so why state it so obviously? And I can't have her criticize JC so pointedly, and she shouldn't say "fucking" so soon.

I also wrote the scene where Fred shows up. I describe him as "mid-twenties, with a tennis-ball haircut, leather jacket, and guitar case over his shoulder." His mind should be several places at once;

often he may seem to talk in non sequiturs.

Change Fred to Gerard.

I just wrote a taping scene between Ann and Gerard. It's pretty raunchy. I don't think Ann would be capable of a lot of the stuff I wrote.

I'm thinking about the following people for the following roles:

Joe Chrest as the husband.
David Jensen as the friend.
Ann Hamilton as the wife.
Megan Austin as the sister.

Maybe there is someone else in the LSU drama department who would be right for Gerard. I'll have to check. Of course, none of the above-mentioned *know* that I'm thinking about them for these roles. Best not to tell until there's something definite.

That's enough for today. If I hang out in the master bedroom too long, my family is going to get suspicious. I mean, it's Christmas Eve, I'm supposed to be enjoying myself, right? Besides, my hand is tired (from writing, you perverts).

25 DEC 87

Again, at my father and stepmother's house, and again I sequester myself in the master bedroom.

* * *

M
It was very exciting. He asked me all sorts of questions and I just answered them.

ANN
What kinds of questions?

M
About sex. All of them were about sex.

ANN
You're kidding me, you answered questions about sex? How could you do that?

                              M

It was easy.

                             ANN

What did he ask you?

                              M

Just stuff. I don't want to say.

                             ANN

Oh, you can have your sexual life recorded on videotape by
someone you barely know, but you won't tell your sister
what you said?

                              M

It's just stuff I don't want to repeat. I got it out of my system,
and that's it.

                             ANN

Did he ask you take your clothes off?

                              M

No.

                             ANN

Did you take your clothes off?

                              M

Yes.

                             ANN

Why?

                              M

Because I wanted to.

                             ANN

Why did you want to?

                              M

Because I wanted him to see my body.

ANN

Jesus Christ, Megan, who knows where that tape is going to
show up. He could be bouncing it off a satellite or something. There could be some horny old men in Brazil whack-
ing off to your tits.

M

I don't care. I don't think he would do that, anyway.

ANN

And he never touched you?

M

Never. I asked him to, but he wouldn't. He told me to touch
myself, so I did.

ANN

What do you mean . . . please . . . don't tell me you mastur-
bated in front of this guy.

M

Yes.

ANN

You are in trouble.

M

What are you talking about?

ANN

I can't believe you did that.

M

Why?

ANN

You don't even know him.

M

I feel like I do.

ANN

That doesn't mean you do. You can't possibly trust this
person.

M

But I do. I do trust him, I think he's honest.

ANN

An honest deviant. Well, I've heard everything now.

M

I asked him if I could see some other tapes of his and he said
no, he'd promised each one that he wouldn't show them to
anybody.

ANN

So he's got this catalogue of women masturbating? Doesn't
that make you feel a little weird? Or generic?

M

No. I don't know what anybody else did, or if they're all
women, even. I did what I did, and it's between me and him.

*   *   *

Also wrote the scene where Gerard asks M if he can tape her. Initially,
this was two scenes, but I think they'll work better combined.

*   *   *

DJ

Does it bother you? I mean, not being able to have an erection around other people?

GERARD

No. Man is incapable of rational thought while in the throes
of an erection, and at least I am able to keep my stupidity
to myself in that regard. A man who is sexually aroused is
barely more than an animal. Less, in some cases. I have no

GERARD *(cont.)*

desire to reveal myself to another person under those cir-
cumstances. That's why I no longer drink, take drugs, or lie.
Every decision one makes is important, and one's mind
must be clear.

DJ

Are you self-conscious?

GERARD

No. You are.

DJ

How do you know?

GERARD

Any halfway observant person could see that. When you are
in public you are convinced others are looking at you.
When you walk down the street, you are concentrating so
hard on walking in just the proper fashion that you trip.
You think the first thing people notice about you is your
thinning hair. And you know what?

DJ

What?

GERARD

You're absolutely right. America wants bright, even teeth,
big breasts, a perfect tan, large penises, and fast cars. Adver-
tising will go down as the scourge of this century, along
with television.

DJ

Television? How can somebody with a video camera say
that television is bad?

GERARD

I am not making or watching television. I have a monitor,
not a television. It doesn't receive transmissions. It shows
only what I give it.

                              DJ
My therapist said tha—

                           GERARD
Stay out of therapy.

                              DJ
Why?

                           GERARD
What possible problems have you got? There are people out
there who have lost limbs, who are paralyzed, who have
disfiguring diseases or painful burns on their bodies. *They*
manage to live. Besides, never take advice from people you
don't know.

                              DJ
My therapist knows me.

                           GERARD
Have you had sex with your therapist?

                              DJ
Of course not.

                           GERARD
Then your therapist doesn't know you. You can never know
anyone *truly*, but through sex you can get a glimpse.

                              DJ
How would you know?

                           GERARD
I said I don't have sex. I never said I didn't.

                              DJ
You said never take advice from someone you don't know,
right?

                           GERARD
Correct.

DJ

And you say you can't know someone, or get a glimpse, rather, until you've had sex with them, right?

GERARD

You're paraphrasing, but I know what you mean. Yes.

DJ

So since I've never had sex with you, and therefore don't *know* you, then by your own advice I shouldn't take your advice.

GERARD

That's correct. Bit of a dilemma, isn't it?

*   *   *

Actually, that would play better as Gerard and Ann, instead of Gerard and DJ. Is DJ necessary at all? It seems like he overlaps Ann and Gerard too much, like they should be saying what he says. I need to think about this. Gerard talks in platitudes too much; it's really obnoxious. Having an opinion is fine, but this guy is too definitive about shit. So why did I write him like that? I don't know.

*   *   *

DJ

I don't think I want to be in therapy anymore.

DR. F

I see. When did you come to this decision?

DJ

I've been thinking about it for a while. And then I was talking to this guy I know, and he just kind of put things in perspective for me.

DR. F

Who is this person you talked to?

DJ

His name is Gerard.

DR. F

And what did he say to you that helped you to put things in perspective?

DJ

Well, I just think that in the scheme of things, my problems are pretty small, you know? I mean, there are people much worse off than myself who are able to—

DR. F

Are you happy?

DJ

Right now, you mean?

DR. F

In general.

DJ

I don't know.

DR. F

David, I don't know who this Gerard person is, but it sounds like he's been pushing you to get out of therapy. Is that so?

DJ

I guess.

DR. F

Don't get me wrong. Not everyone should be in therapy. I happen to think you are benefiting greatly from the time we've spent together. Gerard may have his own motives for disliking therapy and/or therapists. My guess would be that he has some problems of his own that he is unwilling to deal with, and he would like to see someone else, you for instance, wallow in their situation as he does in his. Do you think that's possible?

                    DJ

I guess.

                  DR. F

You understand you are free to leave therapy at any time?

                    DJ

Yes.

                  DR. F

Do you want to leave?

                    DJ

No.

                  DR. F

Do you think there is more progress to be made?

                    DJ

Yes.

                  DR. F

I'm glad you feel that way, because I feel that way, too.

Pause.

                  DR. F

Now, last week we were discussing your appearance. Have
you made any progress in your feelings toward Mel Gibson?

                    DJ

Oh yeah. I don't think about Mel Gibson anymore.

                  DR. F

That's very encouraging, David.

                    DJ

I think about William Hurt.

                *   *   *

Again, it seems like that would play better with Ann instead of DJ.
She needs to be the way into Gerard, and the movie. Knowing that

instinctively, why did I just write that scene between DJ and the therapist, especially since I definitely think DJ should be dropped? Maybe it can be salvaged and used with Ann.

That's enough for now. Time to be social again. I'm bummed that I didn't have any money to get decent presents for anyone, especially since I think everyone is giving me cash for my trip. I wish they'd stop worrying about whether or not the Buick will make it.

26 DEC 87

ANN
All I could think about this past weekend was garbage, literally garbage. I started obsessing over what happens to all the garbage, I mean, what happens to all of it, we have to run out of space eventually, don't we? This happened to me before when that barge with all the garbage was stranded, because nobody would accept it. I don't know what started it this time.

DR.
What do you do when these moods overtake you?

ANN
Nothing, literally nothing. I try not to do anything that will produce garbage. So obviously we're talking about eating and basic stuff like that. Did you know that the average person produces three pounds of garbage a day?

DR.
No, I didn't.

ANN
That's a lot of garbage. I just don't know where it's all going to go.

DR.
If I recall, the week before last you were obsessing with the families of airline fatalities.

ANN
Yeah, so?

DR.

Do you see a pattern here? In that you seem to obsess solely about negative things that you have no control over?

ANN

Well, I don't know many people who run around thinking compulsively about how happy they are. And if there are such people, I doubt they'd be in therapy. Besides, being happy isn't all that great. Last time I was happy I put on twenty-five pounds. My figure is always at its best when I'm depressed.

DR.

How does Joe feel about this current obsession?

ANN

He hasn't said anything. I haven't told him about it.

DR.

Why not? Are you afraid of his reaction?

ANN

Oh, no. I'm pissed off at him right now because he volunteered to let a friend of his stay with us for a while without clearing it with me.

DR.

Tell me what "pisses you off" about that.

ANN

Well, it's my house, too, I mean, I pay half the rent, and I'm really not up to having one of his frat buddies come stay with us with their fucking handshakes and shit.

DR.

This is someone he went to college with?

ANN

I don't know. He said "school." I assumed he meant college.

DR.

This "visit" notwithstanding, how is your relationship with
Joe?

ANN

Okay, I guess. I mean, things aren't real exciting anymore,
but I guess that's natural. He's seemed different lately. And
I say "seemed" because it may just be me and my obsession
thing.

DR.

Do you have much physical contact with him?

ANN

Well, see, that's kind of the thing, I mean, I've never really
been into sex much, but lately we've hardly been doing it at
all, and it's not that I miss it exactly, but I'm just curious the
way things have slacked off, kind of. I'm sure he wishes *I*
would initiate things once in a while, and I would, except
I never think about it, it doesn't even occur to me, I'm
always thinking about something else. And then the few
times I have thought about it he wasn't around.

DR.

You were alone?

ANN

Yes.

DR.

Did you do anything to relieve yourself?

ANN

You mean did I masturbate? No. I don't masturbate.

DR.

You've never tried?

ANN

I tried. It just seemed stupid. I kept picturing myself just
lying there and it seemed stupid, like monkeys in the zoo,

ANN *(cont.)*
I mean, the idea of me watching myself doing it seemed
really stupid and especially when there's all this stuff going
on in the world and what are we going to do with all the
garbage, you know?

Pause. She shakes her head.

DR.
What is it?

ANN
I'm really not up to having a guest this weekend.

* * *

Finally! I need to follow my own advice more often. *Now* I'm getting
somewhere, although after having written forty pages of stuff, I still
don't know where the damn thing is going. I'll pack for the trip some
more and see if I can get this dinner sequence going.

* * *

Finished the dinner sequence and a scene between Ann and her therapist where she talks about Gerard staying at the house.

* * *

M
So where's he from?

JC
Here.

ANN
He's been living in Philadelphia for nine years.

M
Jesus. Why come back?

ANN

I don't know.

JC

There's no telling why he does what he does. He's turned into a strange character.

ANN

I don't think he's strange.

JC

Just before we went to bed the first night: "Joe, you didn't tell me he was so strange."

ANN

I didn't mean it like you thought. Plus, after talking to him, I don't even think he's strange, really.

JC

What is he now?

ANN

Unusual.

JC

Well, that's much more open to interpretation.

M

What's he look like?

JC

I knew it. You're gonna go after him, right?

M

Joe, get some help. I just asked what he looked like.

JC

Right.

M

Besides, even if I decided to fuck his brains out, what business is it of yours?

ANN

Do you have to say that?

M

What, "fuck his brains out"?

ANN

Yes.

M

Works for me.

ANN

Well, he doesn't strike me as the kind of person that would let you do that, anyway.

M

You underestimate me, Ann. Is he straight?

ANN

I don't know; I guess. Joe, do you know?

JC

He was straight when I knew him. But who knows what nine years in Philadelphia will do to a person.

M

There's one way to find out. Can you arrange for me to meet him somehow?

JC

For God's sake . . .

ANN

Really, Megan, I don't think he's your type.

M

My type? What is this bullshit? I have yet to *meet* my type, much less fuck his brains out.

ANN

I really wish—

JC

Your type is walking around dressed in a hospital gown with a scar on each temple.

M

That means a lot coming from the man who turned attitude into an art form.

JC

It ain't braggin' if you can do it.

JC leaves.

ANN

I don't know if there's really a way for you to meet him.

M

What are you talking about? Do you know where he lives?

ANN

I know the address. I haven't seen it yet.

M

Great. You call him up, tell him you want to see what kind of place he found and does he mind if your sister comes along.

ANN

He doesn't have a telephone.

M

How do you know?

ANN

He told me. He doesn't want one.

M

Jesus. Let me guess: He reads by candlelight, right? Look,
just give me his address, I'll think of a reason to stop by.

ANN

Look. Let me talk to him first.

M

Why? Just give me the address.

ANN

I don't feel right just *giving* you the address so that you can
go over there and . . .

M

And what?

*   *   *

I guess that was another dinner scene. There's a lot of good information there, but somehow I doubt the three of them could sit at the
same table without killing each other. Maybe I can salvage some of
this, or eliminate one of the characters.

More packing. Just the essentials: some choice books, word
processor, and some clothes. The rest of my books and clothes will
stay at my father/stepmother's house. I'm excited about the trip. I like
the idea of leaving someplace.

27 DEC 87

I'm staying at my father/stepmother's house since I'm leaving at 6
A.M. I've just stored the last of my stuff in the garage.

I wrote a quick scene between Ann & M that takes place on the
phone. M wants to know why Ann didn't inform Gerard about M. Ann
is vague about what happened with Gerard. 52 pages.

Just wrote another therapy scene with Ann expressing her dis-
taste for M and sexually obsessed people in general.

Also a scene in which M tells Joe that she can't see him today.

28 DEC 87

At 6 A.M. I hugged my father, got into the Buick, and headed for the coast. As I pulled out of the driveway, anything seemed possible (including my car breaking down in the middle of nowhere).

Drove fourteen hours. After taking a shower, I wrote a scene where M goes to visit Gerard (up to the point where they make the tape; the taping part was already written). Then she leaves.

29–30 DEC 87

Drove twenty hours and arrived around 2 A.M. Los Angeles time. Annette let me into the guest house, since Larry won't be back until the 4th of January. It's actually quite chilly, and I couldn't find the heater or any blankets, so I ended up sleeping in my heavy jacket, fully clothed, on Larry's couch. Auspicious beginnings.

When I awoke I wrote the scene where M calls Joe and insists that he leave work to see her. Also a scene where she climaxes and then abruptly asks Joe to leave. Then I wrote the scene where Ann goes to visit Gerard and finds out what his tapes contain.

I began to think maybe I should be working on the spy thriller for Outlaw, since they're paying me. Instead I wrote the scene where Ann reaches over and touches Joe's penis while he sleeps (should go over her sex-obsessed speech with the therapist). Also a scene where Gerard takes his car to a mechanic.

Feeling guilty, I called Bob Newmyer on the phone and arranged to go see *Good Morning, Vietnam* at the Dome tomorrow.

31 DEC 87 LOS ANGELES

Bob and Deborah Newmyer picked me up and we went to the Cinerama Dome. While we were waiting for the movie to start, I told them I was working on a new spec script and gave them a list of the possible titles:

46:02
8 Millimeter
Charged Coupling Device
Retinal Retention
Mode: Visual

Visual Search
Sex, Lies, and Videotape
Hidden Agendas

Bob said without hesitation that *Sex, Lies* (actually, that looks better lowercase), *sex, lies, and videotape* was by far the best title, or at least the most commercial. Deborah, who is head of development for Amblin, agreed.

After the movie, Bob told me that John Kao will be in town soon, and that we should get together and talk about *Revolver*. We agreed on Sunday afternoon.

Again, knowing that I should do work on *Revolver*, I immediately wrote a scene where M returns to Gerard's apartment and asks to make another tape (this type of refusal to do what I am assigned to do is what made me such an aggressively mediocre student). Also, I wrote the scene of Gerard watching Melissa tape.

*   *   *

Party sequence at somebody's garage apartment.

(use John Mese's place, like in *Winston*)

Lots of people. There is dancing. Joe is acting as though Ann were some date he'd rather take home early. Gerard is drinking club soda. A girl goes into the bathroom. A guy, looking around, follows. After a moment, he comes flying out of the bathroom, obviously pushed. Gerard looks at the various women. Megan is talking in a conspiratorial fashion to some girl; they both keep looking at Gerard. Eventually, the girl comes over to Gerard. Ann watches, though she can't hear what's being said.

GIRL

I hear people do unusual things for your camera.

GERARD

Sometimes.

GIRL

You have it with you?

GERARD

My camera?

She nods.

GERARD

Yes. In my car.

GIRL

Show it to me.

Gerard leads the girl outside. He shows her the rig.

GIRL

Turn it on.

Gerard turns the rig on. A small sun gun blares out at the girl.

GERARD

What's your name?

GIRL

Cynthia.

Intercut between the party and Cynthia gradually disrobing in the alley beside the garage, Gerard's sun gun making her ivory flesh glow. M watches, unseen. Ann moves up to her, intending to speak, when she spots Gerard and the girl. Spill light from the girl's backlit figure plays on Ann's face.

GIRL

The light is warm.

GERARD

Yes.

ANN

Aren't you going to do something?

M

I already did. I introduced them.

ANN

They can't do this here.

M

Why not? Who are they bothering? Besides you.

ANN

I don't like it.

M

Then don't look.

* * *

The theory here is that, like in a Fellini film, interesting things supposedly happen when you get the entire cast in one location. Whether or not that sequence is interesting remains to be scene. Parties are expensive to shoot.

1 JAN 88

Ten Favorites as of today:

> *All the President's Men*
> *Annie Hall*
> *Citizen Kane*
> *The 5,000 Fingers of Dr. T*
> *The Godfather (parts I & II)*
> *A Hard Day's Night*
> *Jaws*
> *Sunset Boulevard*
> *The Third Man*
> *A Thousand Clowns*

* * *

GERARD

Elizabeth?

E

Gerard.

GERARD

How are you?

E

I'm fine, how are you?

GERARD

I'm okay.

E

Are you back in town?

GERARD

For a month now.

E

Were you in Philadelphia the whole time?

GERARD

Yes.

E

Oh, excuse me, Gerard, this is Paul. Paul, this is Gerard, an old friend of mine from school.

PAUL

Gerard, nice to meet you.

Gerard nods and shakes Paul's hand.

E

You look different; it took me a second to recognize you.

GERARD

You look very much the same. I mean that as a compliment.

She laughs.

E

I was going to say . . .

                    GERARD
I don't want to keep you.

                      E
Look, do you have a phone number?

                    GERARD
No, actually, I don't. I don't have a phone.

                      E
Oh. Well. Maybe I'll run into you.

                    GERARD
Maybe. It was nice seeing you.

                      E
Thank you. Take care.

                    GERARD
I will. Bye.

                      E
Bye.

                    PAUL
Nice to have met you, Gerard.

                    GERARD
Thanks. B'bye.

                    *   *   *

Also wrote a scene where Ann interrogates Joe in bed. Also the taping
sequence between Ann and Gerard.
       Up to 81 pages.

2 JAN 88

Finished it today. I wrote a scene between M and Joe that will come
after the bedroom interrogation scene but before the scene where Ann
figures out that Joe is screwing around.

Wrote a speech for Gerard about time that I think should occur in his first scene with Ann.

Wrote the scene where Ann comes home and argues with Joe after being at Gerard's.

* * *

Joe pulls up in front of Gerard's apartment, parking haphazardly. He walks briskly to Gerard's door, opening it without a knock. Gerard looks up surprised. Before he can even react Joe has punched him across the face and pinned him to the floor.

JC

Give me those tapes, you fucker! I want those tapes!

GERARD

You can't have them.

JC

~~Gerar~~ Graham, I swear to God I'll kill you, you better give me those tapes.

GRAHAM

No.

JC

Give me your keys.

GRAHAM

My keys?

JC

Give me your keys!! Your two fucking keys!! Give 'em to me!!

GRAHAM

I'm not going to give you my keys.

Joe takes Graham's hand and breaks his index finger. Graham howls in pain while Joe digs for the keys. Finding them, Joe drags Graham across the floor and throws him into the hallway. Joe shuts the door and locks it. He then goes over to the boxes containing Graham's videotapes and rifles spastically through them until he finds the tapes marked ANN and MEGAN. Debating briefly, he decides on Ann's tape. He fumbles with the equipment, cursing himself. Finally, he gets a tape rolling and an image on the monitor.

In the hallway, Graham is numb with pain. He waves off the attention of a neighbor as Ann's voice begins to emanate from within his apartment.

Joe watches the videotape.

WE GO INSIDE THE TAPE. AFTER WE COME OUT:

Joe exits the apartment. Graham has gone. Joe throws the keys inside and shuts the door.

*   *   *

                    DR.
What is it specifically about the homeless that bothers you?

                    ANN
I don't know, they're just all over the place, you know, you see them on the news and who's to say that couldn't happen to me, I mean, I'm single or going to be and I've been out of the work force for a while and I don't really have a skill to speak of, I mean, these homeless women, you see these programs and they—a lot of them—were career women and stuff, I mean they had great jobs and stuff. I just worry . . . I don't like seeing those kinds of things and it seems like it's everywhere you turn and I've been thinking about it.

*   *   *

Graham driving out of town.

*   *   *

Graham destroying the video equipment (should he? when?).

* * *

Joe's monologue in the office about not being married anymore.

* * *

Young guy hitting on M at the bar.

M

Buddy, the only reason I'd fuck you is to keep you from coming in here again and bothering me. Besides, anybody smoking a cigar that big has got to be compensating for something small.

* * *

That's it for the chronology. I stayed up late writing some things to go in the first third of the film, since I know the characters a little better now.

Done. Now I have to load it into the computer. Larry arrives Monday. He will be the first to read it, followed, I imagine, by Mark and Annette.

Make early reference to origin of Graham's name.

Change Joe to John.

M will be Melissa.

3 JAN 88

Went to discuss *Revolver* with Bob and John Kao. It's an odd feeling to be excited about writing a script I don't want to direct. In order for me not to feel like I'm under contract, Bob and John have agreed to pay me $11,000 to option the script once it's completed. That way we both get what we want. So far they've paid me $8,000, so I'm not kidding when I say that I should be working on this thing. Another thing we agreed upon was that once we get a script that we like, Kevin Reynolds is someone we would approach as a potential director.

Larry returns tomorrow and I can print out the first draft. I got Mark to help me build a title page with his Mac. I think I've decided on *46:02*, despite Bob's enthusiasm for *sex, lies, and videotape* and this nagging feeling that when people figure out that *46:02* is the length of Ann's tape, they will dread actually seeing it, thinking (erroneously but understandably) that the sequence will really be that long.

4 JAN 88

Larry returned and I printed out the script, taking the pages to him as they were printed. He seemed to find it compelling but not without problems. I discussed with him my ideas about making it for $60,000 in 16mm on weekends. I made *Winston,* my last short film, for $7500 working that way, so I figure I can do the same on a proportionally larger scale. I have a meeting tomorrow with Nick Wechsler about *State of Mind,* and I'll ask him about possible ways of financing *sex, lies.* (Yeah, I switched back. Larry said *46:02* was death, and threatened to blackmail me with *Mode: Visual,* which he thought was unequivocally the most pretentious title ever conceived.) Nick knows how to find independent money. This is assuming he likes the script, of course.

With a budget of $60,000 or thereabouts, I must be able to raise some money for this thing. My friend Cary Bonnecaze in Baton Rouge has offered a pretty good chunk of change, so that's a start. I just don't think this script is going to get made in any sort of Hollywood fashion. I need to give Ann Dollard the script tomorrow so she can read it and figure out if there's anyone she can send it out to. She's excited that I'll be in town for a while.

5 JAN 88

I met with Nick and we discussed, among other things, possible financing options for *sex, lies,* including his putting up money personally if the budget stays this low. He seems very enamored, as I am, of just doing it on the quick for cheap.

6–11 JAN 88

Responses to *sex, lies* tend to be more positive than I anticipated. Nick liked it, Ann Dollard (and her assistant and brother, Patrick) liked it, and both are going to send it to a couple of places that finance independent low-budget stuff. Mark and Annette liked it as well (Mark found it arousing, which was interesting), so the ratio so far is pretty good. I started drawing up more detailed budgets. One for $75,000 or so, and one for $200,000 or so.

Guilt forced me to produce 35 pages of *Revolver,* but I wasn't too happy with what I'd written so far, so I didn't show anything to Bob or John Kao.

Nathalie Seaver, an old friend who works for Showtime, called to ask if I want to cut a trailer for a made-for-cable movie they're finishing. I hesitated initially, but I decided to do it, because Nathalie is a good friend and I can always use a couple extra bucks.

12–17 JAN 88

Nathalie and I worked on the trailer, which was for a movie called *Gotham,* starring Tommy Lee Jones and Virginia Madsen. The trailer was for some expo presentation or something. We went through several false starts and re-edits before finally coming up with something that we (and everyone else) were happy with. I'm glad I did it, actually. It was a throwback to days of old when I would come out to L.A. a couple of times a year to re-cut something for Showtime. Nathalie is really the only person from that era still at Showtime, which is regrettable. Things aren't as loose there as they used to be. Oh well.

While working at Showtime on my birthday, Mark, Annette, their kids, and Larry brought me a surprise birthday cake, which was incredibly nice. I feel so awkward in such situations. I mean, I was genuinely moved by what they did, but I didn't know how to show it, and I have this feeling they left thinking I didn't appreciate it, when I really did. I must work on this, especially now that I'm twenty-five. A quarter of a century. And for what?

18–24 JAN 88

A week's worth of waiting for further news/feedback on *sex, lies,* making phone calls, and avoiding work on *Revolver.* I met with Nick again to discuss further financing options. He's got the script to a company that he thinks will be very interested. Ann sent the script to Cassian Elwes at Cinema Group Entertainment, since he was interested in a previous script of mine (*State of Mind,* actually).

Bob, John Kao, and I set up a meeting at New World to discuss *Dead From The Neck Up.* Despite our inability to get it set up, we still like the script a lot. The problem has been that it's set in 1941, and even at a lowball cost of $6 million, nobody wants to take a chance with a "first-time" director.

25–31 JAN 88

Waiting.

I tinkered with what I'd written for *Revolver* but in my heart I'd rather something happened with *sex, lies.* Apropos of that, Bob finally cajoled me into letting him read it. He'd been lightheartedly bugging me about it, and since I've been jerking around on *Revolver,* I felt morally obligated to let him read the thing. I just didn't think it was his kind of piece, and worse, I thought it would really change the way he looked at me. Well, as it turned out, he liked it a lot, which shows how much I know. He said he had to keep reading to find out what was going to happen. I was really quite surprised, especially when he asked if he could get involved with the project. I told him it's an open field, but that there are others with a head start on him. So he's going to pursue some options. Deborah, his wife, couldn't get past page thirty. She said it was too weird. I can understand that.

1–7 FEB 88

Interesting week. I met with Cassian Elwes on Tuesday, and he was very interested in making the film, if he can convince the few people above him that a worthwhile film can be made for $300,000 (that's the current 35mm budget). So that's encouraging.

The *Dead From The Neck Up* meeting at New World was re-scheduled twice, and is now set for next week.

I saw *Julia and Julia* because it was shot on high-definition video (although I thought I detected one or two inserts that looked as though they were shot on film), and it just proves my theory that you can make a bad film in any format.

Larry and I saw *The Unbearable Lightness of Being* on Sunday, which I liked very much, although once the film moved into the country I wasn't as interested, and I wasn't particularly moved by the dog dying. Larry stood in line for popcorn behind Helena Bonham Carter, which was pretty exciting. Anyway, I didn't read Kundera's book, but I don't think that should ever be a prerequisite for liking or understanding a film. Books and films are obviously very different media, and unless you're going to hand out free copies of the novel in the lobby and tell people to come back when they've read it, I think the film better work on its own terms, as a film. Certainly *Great Expectations* works without having read the book, as does *Jaws.* How's that for a double bill?

8–14 FEB 88

This was the week that is. Suddenly, there are three people interested in *sex, lies,* not including Cassian Elwes, who had to pass. In order of appearance: J. Paul Higgins, an aspiring producer and old friend of mine from *Games People Play,* offered to option the script with a friend of his, Hank Palmieri. They have access to some private money (a safe combination, perhaps?) and feel they can raise cash very quickly. Bob Newmyer made a contact with a guy he knows at RCA/ Columbia Home Video, Larry Estes, and *he* is very interested, although he thinks black-and-white will be a problem for his boss (but not for Larry personally. He and I spent a great deal of the meeting discussing *The Last Picture Show* and other mutual favorites). He will call us soon. Then on Friday, Nick Wechsler took me to see a guy named Morgan Mason at a company called Musifilm, who says *he* wants to make the movie, and he doesn't care if it's in black-and-white. Furthermore, he says his boss doesn't care either. I liked Morgan very much, so by week's end I was exhilarated and confused.

Finally had the New World meeting. Bob, John Kao, and Jeff Silver (who did all the budgets) joined me in meeting with Randy Levenson, who said he liked *Dead From The Neck Up* very much, but didn't know whether or not he could sell the higher-ups. I am used to this.

Worked on second draft of *sex, lies.* Still avoiding *Revolver* for no real reason.

15–21 FEB 88

Well, basically, it looks like I'll be going with Musifilm, for two reasons. Larry Estes couldn't talk his boss into black-and-white, and while J. Paul and Hank could surely raise the money, I don't think they could raise it fast enough for my taste at this particular moment in time. I'm somewhat bummed that it won't happen with Outlaw/ RCA Columbia, because I really like all the people involved on that end, but hey, I like Nick and Morgan as well, and at the meeting on Thursday I was assured that I can have all of the creative controls I'm seeking. The budget now stands at $500,000 (it's become like the Andromeda Strain; every time you look away it gets bigger. The question is, will it get better?).

22–28 FEB 88

Busy week. Finished second draft of *sex, lies,* had a whole bunch of meetings at Musifilm, and drew up a lot of budgets. The second draft is only slightly different, with the tone being affected more than anything else. I cut the party sequence out, because it seemed somewhat tasteless (and expensive. Don't ask me which was the main reason for cutting it). I guess the biggest change was the ending, which nobody was really satisfied with, and frankly, when I read through the script again, I didn't find it emotionally satisfying, either. I wanted Ann and Graham to make contact. I think a lot of it has to do with the fact that I just feel better now than I did two months ago, meaning I'm not so quick to offer up a "That's just the way it goes" ending. I particularly think it would be unfair for Ann to make no progress. She goes through a lot, and she's sharp enough to learn from it. So I just played up the humor a little more and let Ann and Graham make some sort of emotional bond. The film is very talky, though, and that worries me.

Musifilm is trying to tie me up after the movie with some sort of multi-picture option clause, where they get first look at anything I write and pay me an obscenely small stipend. Needless to say, Ann Dollard is not very happy about that, but otherwise things are going well.

J. Paul asked me to write a short (fifteen-page) script for him to submit to the Discovery Program. If they like the script, he'll get to direct it. I agreed to do it, even though I don't have the time. Feeling guilty, I guess.

29 FEB–13 MAR 88

Broke the script down for scheduling, had more production meetings. During the day I work out of Mike Curb's office, he who owns Musifilm. He is the former Lt. Governor of California, and aggressively Republican, from what I gather, in addition to having produced some hit records (a Gold Record of some version of "You Light Up My Life" hangs on the wall beside me). It's a strange vibe, but I cope. I brought John Hardy on board to line produce the film. We always talked hopefully of getting an independent feature made, and I'm psyched (a Bob Newmyer word) that we're getting the chance. I started making some calls to crew members in Louisiana. I ordered 100,000 feet of black-and-white negative from Kodak. We'll have to pay C.O.D. to get a break on the cost, because a price increase is imminent. Sounds like there's going to be a writers' strike. Curious as to how that will affect us. Maybe we can get everything signed before the strike starts. We've set May 2 as start of principal photography (same day *Jaws* started shooting!).

14–20 MAR 88

Morgan got a tip on a casting person, Deborah Aquila, so we sent her a script in New York. Morgan, Nick, and I called her on the phone and she said she was fifteen pages in and thought the script was laugh-out-loud funny. The three of us exchanged worried looks and told her to call us back when she was done reading. She telephoned an hour later, noticeably subdued. She also agreed to cast the film, accepting the less-than-massive sum we offered. I'm due to go to New York on the 27th and begin casting.

Musifilm would like to try and get some recognizable actors for the movie in order to better secure their investment, and have approved additional funds (up to $250,000) for this purpose. That's fine with me. My feeling is that I would have to make an unwatchable piece of shit not to return a half-million-dollar investment, but if they are willing to pay for some recognizable names, I think that's great, because now I can go after Elizabeth McGovern for the role of Ann.

24 MAR 88

John Hardy flew in today so that he and I could make formal presentations to the insurance company. Everything seemed to go fine. Morgan is insisting that I spend time with the Musifilm person in New York, Nancy Tenenbaum. I will meet her next week.

25 MAR 88

Preliminary casting. I think casting is going to be weird, in the sense that I have the feeling I'll see a lot of good actors, and the decision-making could be difficult, especially since it's an ensemble piece. What am I complaining about? I'm getting to make the film, right? So shut up.

28 MAR 88 NEW YORK

I met with Davian Littlefield, who manages Andie MacDowell and
some other actors that I'll be seeing. Davian is a good friend of Nick's
and she is pushing Andie, who is obviously beautiful, but nothing I've
seen in her work indicates she could *carry* a movie, which is what this
role requires. Shit, at least she wants to do it. Elizabeth McGovern's
agent hated the script so much she wouldn't show it to Elizabeth, so
unless we can figure out a way to circumvent the agent (Elizabeth is
doing a play in New York right now), I'll just have to look elsewhere.
We're trying to get Aidan Quinn for Graham. I think he's great.

30 MAR–1 APR 88

Casting. A new person every fifteen minutes for eight hours. I try to
make a connection with everybody that comes in, try to make them
feel like it was worth their time. One day I was sitting outside Deb's
office while she was screening some actors and since nobody knew
who I was I got to hear some unsolicited, unexpurgated comments
about the script.

ACTOR 1: So did you read the whole thing, or just sides?

ACTOR 2: I read the whole thing.

ACTOR 1: Me too. I don't know, what'd you think?

ACTOR 2: I don't know. Weird.

ACTOR 1: It's just so *negative*, you know? What's the point? I mean,
who wants to see that?

ACTOR 2: Yeah.

ACTOR 1: And why make it a movie? It doesn't seem like a movie, it
seems like a play to me. Didn't it read like a play to you?

ACTOR 2: I guess. I don't know.

The best thing that happened was that I met Nancy Tenenbaum and
she was every bit as great as Morgan insisted she was. She's been in

on all the casting, and we've been having a great time.

Elizabeth McGovern is out. We just couldn't get to her. Linda Kozlowski's agent hated the script. Aidan Quinn passed. We've got a script to Kyle MacLachlan's agent. The really big news was Andie MacDowell. She fucking blew me away with her audition. She had truly inspired choices, things that weren't written, which is risky on two levels: One, as I said, doing things that aren't in the script is always dangerous, and two, if you don't totally nail it, you won't even get a callback. You might not even be allowed to finish your audition. She was amazing. It was just her and I in the room, and when I came out and told Deb and Nancy that I thought Andie was the best I'd seen, they looked at each other like "Uh-oh, Steven fell for the model." I'm convinced that when Andie comes in for callbacks with the tape machine rolling, I will be vindicated. I don't know what she's been doing the last three years, but it worked.

Also, looks solid for Timothy Daly as John. I like him very much, and he likes the material.

Ron Vawter is a lock for the therapist. He initially came in as a possible Graham if we decided to go older, but three lines into the audition I stopped everything and turned to Deb Aquila and said "He's the therapist." She looked at me as though the same thought had just occurred to her and we decided on the spot.

4–6 APR 88

Callbacks. The consensus after taping callbacks is Andie MacDowell for Ann to go with Timothy Daly, and probably Laura San Giacomo as Cynthia, although Nicoletta Scorsese was interesting as well (assuming I can cast an unknown for Cynthia. Right now there's a script going to Jennifer Jason Leigh). The role of Graham is turning out to be difficult. Kyle MacLachlan passed, and the only person I saw in New York that fits in the range we're in was a guy named Brad Greenquist (he played the killer in *The Bedroom Window* with his hair dyed red). He's brilliant, but Musifilm wants a recognizable name for Graham, so for now, I'm at a loss. It is decided that I will return to L.A. and find a Graham. I heard that James Spader is interested. We had sent a script to Helen Slater, and her agent is also Spader's agent, and she gave Spader the script, thinking he might like it. Apparently, he did, and although I'm not sure he's really right for Graham, he is well known, and he is a good actor, so what the hell.

8 APR 88 LOS ANGELES

James Spader read for me today. It was funny; he came over to Mark and Annette's house and read with Annette (who is an actress), and he was great. When he first walked in, he said hello and that he really wanted to be in the movie, which made me feel good. And as I said, I was ambivalent when his name was first brought up. He'd been very good in everything I'd seen him in, I just hadn't seen him in anything like this, and being the neophyte dilettante that I am, I assumed that if he hadn't done it, he couldn't do it. I assumed the same thing about Andie, and look what happened. From now on, I'll assume an actor can do anything I require until he/she proves otherwise.

Nick and I are scheduled to meet with Morgan on Monday. We heard vague rumblings in New York that Musifilm is getting nervous about black-and-white.

9 APR 88

Saw *D.O.A.* at the Cinerama Dome with Larry. The film was exceedingly stylish, but left me cold (amazing credit sequence, though). It just sounded to me like people saying stuff that people say in the movies, not real life. I know, it wasn't a documentary, I just like the feeling (or the illusion, rather) that the conversations on-screen are actually occurring as I watch them.

11 APR 88

Black Monday.

Musifilm has officially bailed. Fuck!!

They choked on black-and-white. Now we've got to figure out a way to keep the cast together while we shop the project around, assuming we don't get sued, since we made pay-or-play offers to the actors. Goddammit. I already sold the Buick to Aaron! I called John Hardy to give him the bad news. Nick and I are trying to convince Nancy Tenenbaum to leave Musifilm and come with us to work on setting the movie up somewhere else. Shit.

Morgan, understandably, was crushed and horrified, since this obviously wasn't his decision. I felt bad for him, but worse for us. They paid for lunch.

I called Bob Newmyer to tell him that if he wants to join forces and try to set the film up we'd be happy to have his help. He said he'd love to.

12–26 APR 88

Shopped *sex, lies* to everyone that we could think of, with no success. Nobody will touch black-and-white. I'm running out of money. I mostly sit on Larry's couch and talk on the phone to Nancy T. about script revisions (she did leave Musifilm) and listen to Elvis Costello's "Out of Our Idiot" all day. Things don't look so hot. There aren't many companies left to approach. Every day Nick is on the phone to the actors' agents trying to hold the cast together, and I pitch in when I can. Larry Estes at RCA/Columbia said the package looks better than ever, but he still can't sell his boss on you-know-what.

27 APR 88

Two interesting meetings today. First, Bob Newmyer and I went to Nick Wechsler's office and formalized a partnership of sorts. It's not really a business contract or anything, just an agreement of how the picture should be split up. So as of this writing, it's Bob, Nick, Nancy, and John Hardy.

Second, I went over to IRS World Media, which is the film division of Miles Copeland's music empire. I met with Paul Colichman, who had gotten the script from Ann Dollard, and he said flat out that IRS is interested, but with two provisos: One, the budget has to be $500,000 (there goes my cast), and two, the film must be shot in Los Angeles (there goes . . . something intangible. I feel strongly that the film should be shot outside of a recognizable urban area, and I'd like to go home, where I feel comfortable). He said he needed an answer in 48 hours, because they need to make a decision this week on which film they will make. I told him I would give him an answer in 48 hours. He's also not completely sold on black-and-white, and inquired whether or not I could mix it with color. Again, I said I'd think about it. This is a legitimate offer to get the film made, so I'll have to weigh it carefully.

I've been thinking a lot about the whole black-and-white thing. The tone of the film has changed somewhat with the new draft, in an attempt to bring out some humor, and so maybe black-and-white isn't appropriate anymore. Also, it's quite plain that I am not Woody Allen, and therefore don't have the clout to insist and get my way. Plus, I was talking to a friend of Bob Newmyer's, Mark Balsam, and he said he could understand why I would want to shoot in black-and-white, but that people would then be judging the style before the content. That really stuck in my mind, because I don't want anything distracting people from the performances or the story.

It looks more and more like I'll have to make the film in color or not at all.

28 APR 88

Paul Colichman called me today and said he needed an answer. I told him my answer, regrettably, was no. He then started yelling at me over the phone, saying "You'll never raise a million dollars! You're operating out of fear! And don't come back here and expect me to say yes! You get one chance! You're making a big mistake!" I told him I hoped he was wrong. He said he knew he was right. Wow.

Ann called me ten minutes later, obviously unnerved, and said, "What did you say to him?" I told her that I said no, thank you. I don't know why the guy yelled at me. What was I supposed to do, say "Yeah, you're right, I really do want to work with you" after I've been reamed verbally? And as for going back there, certainly I would never go back, for fear of receiving further abuse. It just seemed like bad business to me. Pat Dollard said the guy called me "a clown." Now I guess I have to get the film made, JUST TO PROVE A POINT.

It looks like Morgan will remain on the film, probably as an executive producer. It's a difficult situation, and I have mixed feelings. On the one hand, I want him involved because I like him, he's smart, he'll help the project, and he knows everybody. As a matter of fact, he and Nancy T. have been pushing a guy at Virgin Vision, Mike Watts, to purchase the foreign rights, and having a deal in place for foreign rights would help us tremendously. On the down side, he still works for Musifilm, a company that I don't have mixed feelings about. Ultimately, it's my feeling that the pros far outweigh the cons, so I think he'll definitely stay on board.

I met a guy, Cliff Martinez, who I think I will ask to compose the music for *sex, lies* should the film get made (am I supposed to say *when* the film gets made?). He's working with Mark and John P. on some source cues for *Alien Nation* (Mark is the supervising sound editor on the film), and I really liked what I heard. I talked to him for a little while, and he seemed like a really nice guy. He's the drummer in a punk band called The Dickies, and he's very enthused about

writing film music. My gut says he would do a good job. Let's hope
I get the opportunity to find out.

2 MAY 88

Once upon a time, we were going to start shooting today.

5 MAY 88

Lost Tim Daly, then got him back. It's been difficult keeping the cast
together, since all the agents think we're full of shit since the money
fell through. So we're still getting on the phone a couple of times a
week, trying to keep everyone enthused, and praying privately that no
one will get work that would conflict with *sex, lies.*

6 MAY 88

Let it be known that on this day I decided that we should make the
movie in color.

9 MAY 88

It's official, we're going to go with Larry Estes and RCA/Columbia. He
has to get approval, of course, but he is very passionate about the
project and the financial projections that he and Bob have done indicate that in a worst-case scenario (an unspeakably shitty film, which
I *am* capable of), RCA/Columbia could generate enough sales ultimately (worldwide, cable, etc.) to cover a cash budget of $1.1 million.
We agree on a $100,000 deferment on top of that. Nancy T. is pushing
Mike Watts at Virgin to make the foreign deal, so she and I talk daily,
usually at great length, about that situation. I try to keep occupied by
reading and avoiding other forms of writing besides tinkering with
sex, lies.

    I feel bad that I've been on Larry's couch for so long. We're
actually having a lot of fun, staying up to watch "The Honeymooners"
every night at midnight, and then talking through the wall with the
lights out like a couple of girls at camp or something. When I first told
Larry I was coming to Los Angeles for a while, he said I could stay
for a month or two, and here it's been five. I constantly feel that other
people treat me better than I treat them. Friendship-wise, I mean.
Surely I can do something about this.

10–16 MAY 88

More waiting, albeit of a different nature.

John Kao wants Outlaw to option a book called *The Last Ship*, and he gave me a copy to read, in the hopes that I would serve as a good-natured mediator between himself and Bob. You see, Bob loves the book also, he just feels its size is counter to the whole concept of Outlaw, which is to make low-to-medium-budget independent features, primarily comedic. Unfortunately for Bob, I flipped over the book. I literally couldn't put it down until I'd finished it. Unfortunately for John, that didn't sway Bob, and when John said he loved the book so much that he was going to option it personally, I, unfortunately for John, said I thought that was a great idea (this option will cost him serious money). The plan is to try a get a big-name director attached. Shit, I wish there were some way for me to get involved. Whenever we bandy names of potential directors about, inside I think *I want to do it, don't let them touch it, they'll screw it up.* Unfortunately for me, my interest doesn't mean shit.

17 MAY 88

Annette and I worked a scam for Larry's birthday today. I bought Larry a new couch (on my Amex card. I must be getting confident) to replace his old foam thing (okay, so it's a present for me, too), and while Larry was working at Weddington, Annette and I put the new couch into the guest house and took the old one to Weddington and put it in the dumpster outside the front door so Larry would see it on his way to lunch. As it turned out, he did finally see it, but his reaction was somewhat more subdued than we desired. He apparently smiled, shook his head and said "Soderbergh."

I think it's a very comfortable couch, and it really matches the carpet well.

18 MAY–9 JUNE 88

Waiting for final approval. Larry Estes got his boss to say yes, but there are several levels of approval above that, apparently. At one point I heard Bob say "The guy from G.E. is looking at it." G.E.? How did they get involved?

I saw *Call Me,* which contained some very blunt sexual language, and got me thinking about how far to go with the language in *sex, lies.*

I mean, some of the lines in this movie made me wince, and I'm pretty open about that stuff. I think I'll go back through the current draft of *sex, lies* and check for potential wince factors.

There has been some interest in trying to get a fourth "name" for Cynthia, which leaves me feeling ambivalent. Over and above the fact we don't have the money, I'd really like to give Laura the break. Fortunately, since Jennifer Jason Leigh passed, Larry Estes is inclined to agree with me, so I really think we'll go with Laura.

I saw *Big*, which reminded me of a pseudo-Tom Hanks story. In late '85, I had a meeting with Mary Ann Page, who (at that time) was Hanks's development person. She really liked *Crosstalk,* which is basically about a guy who uproots his family. She said it was perfect material for Hanks, except for the fact that his management didn't want him to appear in films wherein his character had children, even though Hanks had (and has) a young son of his own. She was clearly frustrated by this edict, as was I, obviously. So that's my big Tom Hanks story.

10–12 JUNE 88

I had been getting headaches while reading *The Fatal Shore,* and since I loved what I was reading, I knew it wasn't the material. Well, I got an eye exam, and lo, I have an astigmatism. Glasses are forthcoming.

Saw *The Presidio.* My favorite part was the trailer for *Tucker: The Man and His Dream.*

Saw and loved *Who Framed Roger Rabbit?* Mind-blowing. I predict it will make a lot of money. Stop the presses, right?

15 JUNE 88

Flashing green light!! Larry Estes says it will happen. I'm trying to remain calm, which means not calling anyone for fear of bringing on a jinx.

Saw *Wings of Desire,* which was amazing. I felt like I was floating when I left the theater. It's the kind of film that not only couldn't be made in America, but *shouldn't* be made in America.

16–20 JUNE 88

Indulging in the mental equivalent of nail-biting. Had a meeting with the bond company, which was pretty interesting. Basically, they make you jump through a few intellectual hoops and ask lots of "what if?" questions. The guy we're dealing with, Robert Mintz, is really nice. He said actually, first-time feature directors are, in his experience, notoriously responsible. He said it's the second-timers they have trouble with. I will remember this.

I have decided that Steven Brill, a writer with a project in development at Outlaw, will play the barfly. He and I have been hanging around the office for months and he jokingly asked if I had a part for him in *sex, lies* and I said, Yeah, I do. He's perfect for the part. His script, *Meet Your Match,* is really funny, and I predict it will get made into a movie (boy, a lot of predictions lately). He agreed to give me a role in *Meet Your Match* to make the deal even, and I think that's fair. The question is, will he have enough clout to get me in his film? I mean, I'm the director on *sex, lies,* but what if the eventual director of *Meet Your Match* doesn't want me in the movie? Well, if it comes to that, it'll be a good problem for Steve to have.

21 JUNE 88

GREEN LIGHT!! WE'RE ON!! No fooling, this is the real thing, accept no substitutes. Many, many, many phone calls to make. We start principal photography August 1.

Some bad news. We lost Tim Daly. He took a TV series ("Almost Grown"), and even though the writers' strike has pushed his commitment back, he can't do it. We're on the prowl for a new John. Outlaw, by the way, signed the interim agreement with the Writers Guild in order that we continue.

24 JUNE 88

Now I'm having trouble with Laura. Or rather, her agency. They don't want her to do the movie, thinking it will be exploitive at best (this is the same agency that handles Elizabeth McGovern). I talked to Laura, and she wants to do the movie, she's just trying to ascertain from me whether or not any nudity will be required. The best I can do is tell her that I don't think there will be, but I'm not positive. I mean, I've had long conversations with Nancy T. about this, and her feeling is that women, in general, are put off by female nudity in films. I don't doubt that, and I'm a big believer in equanimity. We all know it's not the same for a guy to take his shirt off, so if we're talking about below-the-waist, I don't think it would be fair to ask that of the girl and not the guy, and what guy will do that? The bottom line is I will do whatever is appropriate, and whereas I think that means no nudity, I'm not 100% positive. I got the feeling Laura wishes I could be more definitive, if only so she could put her agency at ease. They really don't want her to do the film. We agreed to talk in a few days.

On the male-actor front, it looks like I'm going to Seattle to see James Spader. He wants to do the movie, he just wants to talk about a few problems he has with the script. It's imperative that he do the film, and he and I have talked over the phone about possible changes. His comments are all very lucid and constructive, although I think we're both being overly accommodating, in the sense that neither of us wants to alienate the other.

28 JUNE 88 SEATTLE

Jimmy (he prefers Jimmy) and I met for several hours in the afternoon to discuss script changes. The main area of concern for him seemed to be the motivation for both Graham's severe withdrawal from people and his return to Baton Rouge. We came up with a backstory involving a child that Graham had fathered with Elizabeth that turned out to be retarded and led to Graham's eventually abandoning Elizabeth due to an inability to deal with the child. He seemed satisfied, so I'm hoping everything will now proceed apace.

Jimmy suggested that I contact Peter Gallagher about the role of John. Jimmy had just spent time with him at a Sundance workshop, and said Peter was great to work with and very talented. I'm definitely interested, but I'll have to run it by Larry Estes, and I guess Nancy T. will have to run it by Mike Watts as well. Virgin has agreed to make a deal for overseas, but the actual negotiations are proceeding slowly. I think both RCA and Virgin want pens to hit paper simultaneously. We have to move quickly, though, if we're going to make the start date. I've got to start looking seriously for a DP.

2 JUL 88

This morning I got a call from J. Paul Higgins saying that Ann Dollard had been badly injured in a horseback-riding accident. I immediately went out to the hospital, where a large contingent of friends had already begun to gather, along with the immediate family. I found the whole thing very disorienting. I went in to see her, and she'd obviously taken a terrible fall (I was told that her brain stem was crushed). She's in a coma, and even though I knew it was her, it didn't seem like her, perhaps because her facial features were distorted from the swelling. I held her hand, which was very warm. Preliminary testing showed no brain activity whatsoever. After speaking with Pat and several mutual friends for a couple of hours, I left, still not able to connect Ann with the person I saw hooked up to all those machines, and frustrated by my inability to be deeply upset. I just felt numb. I thought about the day in mid '85 when I first met Ann and she looked at my reel and agreed to represent me. "How old are you?" she asked. I told her I was twenty-two. "A baby," she said.

3 JUL 88

I met with Peter Gallagher and decided to cast him as John. We talked for a couple of hours, and his ideas for the role were great. Peter's had an interesting career. His first film was *The Idolmaker*, which opened right when the actors' strike started, so instead of offers rolling in he sat around unemployed for months afterward. We agreed it was just as well that he learned right off the bat that you can't count on anything in this business.

4 JUL 88

They took Ann off the machines today. She was thirty-two years old.

5 JUL 88

Had a meeting with Toyomichi Kurita, who shot *The Moderns*. I liked him a great deal, and I hoped that he would agree to shoot the film. I called his agent and there seemed to be a potential conflict with another film Toyomichi is probably going to do with Alan Rudolph. After several phone calls with Rudolph's people and Toyomichi's agent, it became apparent that he couldn't do *sex, lies*. Toyomichi and his agent both strongly recommended a guy named Walt Lloyd, who has operated for Toyomichi and John Seale, in addition to shooting two films for Albert Pyun. Toyomichi really said great things about Walt, so it sounded like a lead worth following. The agent is sending a copy of *Down Twisted* to me tomorrow, and I'll meet with Walt the following day.

6 JUL 88

Staggering amounts of phone calls. Now that we've been green-lighted, we need a check so we can start this fuggin' thing on Aug. 1. John Hardy and I continue to draw up new and improved budgets, shifting money around to accommodate continually changing developments with personnel and equipment.

I watched *Down Twisted,* and it looked fine, it just didn't look anything like I imagine *sex, lies* should look. But past experience has taught me that I shouldn't assume that Walt can't provide exactly what I'm looking for.

7 JUL 88

I met with Walt Lloyd, and my gut says go with him. He liked the script very much, and we seem to have similar ideas about how the film should look. Additionally, Walt is willing to work with a crew that I've already hired and that he obviously has never worked with before, which is a difficult thing to ask a DP to do (especially when the DP is operating as well). Some cinematographers would refuse, and rightfully so. I guess we'll see if my gut feelings pay off.

I leave for Baton Rouge on the twelfth. Still waiting on the first check from RCA/Columbia. John Hardy and I are finding that it is very difficult to preproduce a movie with no money. I'll bet it's been done, though, and on movies much larger than ours.

It's weird, because RCA/Columbia is in the driver's seat, so the contract is pretty stacked on their side, although the profit-division stuff is actually quite favorable for both sides. They have final cut, and they can change the title and make a sequel and/or a TV series without my approval (I have right of first refusal on the sequel/series thing). The film has to be between 85 and 105 minutes in length and "accurately reflect the approved screenplay." So what it comes down to is my relationship with Larry Estes, which I feel is a good one. My gut feeling (here we go again) is that as long as I'm on schedule and budget, I'll be left alone. Title changes have been discussed, but none of us can come up with anything as intriguing (one of Nick's favorite words) as the one we have.

Returning to Baton Rouge this time will be much different than when I returned in late '81. I had come back a wizened failure, which is better than an unwizened failure, I suppose. The intervening years have been full of illumination, and in many ways I don't think I would have been ready before now to make this film (or any film of real substance, for that matter).

I've offered my friends Aaron and Alex jobs on the film, and they will also share a rented apartment with me in Baton Rouge. I'm not sure exactly what they will be doing, but they are both the kind of people that excel in whatever they set their minds to, and it'll be fun having them along for the ride.

8–11 JUL 88

Laura will do the movie. I agreed to contractually guarantee her that she won't have to do any nudity. I felt I had to do this in order for her to feel good about doing the movie, so it was worth it to me. I don't think we'll need any nudity anyway.

Met with Steve New, the negative cutter, to discuss how to best transcribe my video edit list so he can accurately conform the workprint. Transferring the printed takes to video and cutting the movie on that medium will save us a lot of time, and some money, since I won't need an assistant. Weddington has agreed to let Larry Blake cut and mix all the sound in their new multi-track room, which is interlocked with video. It's a tape finish on this film, folks.

12 JUL 88 BATON ROUGE

Back home. I'm staying at my father/stepmother's house until I find an apartment for Aaron, Alex, and myself. Still no check from RCA/Columbia. Bob has been spending many long days over there trying to get the contracts sewed up. It's very complicated, because the Virgin contract is tied to this one very intricately, and Nancy T. is constantly getting new demands from both ends. For example, let's say Virgin offers to pay 60% upon principal photography, 20% upon delivery, and 20% upon first foreign video release. RCA/Columbia may counter with 80/10/10, or whatever. Needless to say, the faxes are flying. Actually, I'm stunned that Virgin is going in on the deal. I've never met or spoken with Mike Watts, he's never seen any of my short films, and to my knowledge he's only read the first draft, which clearly had problems. I guess Nancy T. and Morgan have nasty photos of him with farm equipment or something.

Production offices will be at Cranch, Lemoine, and Hardy, the ad agency John Hardy shares ownership of with Sonny Cranch and Bill Lemoine, both of whom I've worked with before as well, when I was employed by Video Park, Inc. in '83/84. They're funny guys, and they've already been helping John and me out a lot on the film.

Spoke to David Foil, who I decided will play the small role of John's colleague. He's the entertainment critic at the Baton Rouge paper, and we've been close friends for a long time. He wants to leave Baton Rouge, and I am continually encouraging him to do so. He knows more about music, theater, and film than anyone I've ever met, so it's been a great friendship for me to have, since I can soak up all this information that he's gathered over the years. I don't know what he's gotten out of it. Vicarious thrills, I'm sure. Really though, our tastes are remarkably similar, with some minor exceptions: he likes *Blow Out* (I don't), and I like *The Gods Must Be Crazy* (he doesn't). Everything else we pretty much agree upon. That's a good ratio, I think.

14 JUL 88

Getting crew together. I think we've got an art director. Her name is Joanne Schmidt, and she worked as an assistant on *Everybody's All-American*, so she knows where to go in Baton Rouge to get stuff cheap. David Jensen, who I wanted to act in the first incarnation of *sex, lies,* will be best boy (he also played the lead in my last short film). Phil Beard and Michael Charbonnet, who also worked on my last short, will be gaffer and 1st asst. camera, respectively. Paul Ledford will be the production mixer, and Stephen Tyler, fellow filmmaker and friend of four years, will be the boom man. Ben Williams, who went to my high school and is also a filmmaker (I acted in two of his short films, believe it or not), will probably assist Paul and Stephen. It's likely that Aaron will end up in the art department, probably as prop master. The P.A. that shows the most initiative will probably be drafted as 2nd A.D. At this point John Hardy is supposed to be the A.D., but he and I are both concerned that it will be too much for one person. He said he would check around tomorrow for a decent A.D. that will work for cheap. Jimmy Spader's wife, Vicki, will be set decorator, which is very convenient for us and, I imagine, for Jimmy.

John Hardy is desperately trying to get all of the necessary contracts together for the bond company, who (in theory) could shut us down if they aren't satisfied. I, for example, have yet to sign a director's agreement, and I'm sure John hasn't signed anything, either. For the record, I'm getting Writer's Guild minimum for the script (around $21,000), and $16,000 to direct and edit. Hey, I've got nobody to blame, I drew up the budget. It is somewhat amusing to John and me that we are getting the same salaries we were getting when the film was budgeted at $500,000. Somewhat.

Bob called late to say we got the first check!! It will arrive by courier tomorrow morning (that will probably cost $200 right there). John Hardy is greatly relieved. He'd been keeping the *sex, lies* account open with a deposit of six dollars.

15–24 JUL 88

Busy week. Walt arrived, and he joined John Hardy, myself, Joanne Schmidt, and Vicki Spader in the hunt for locations. At one point Joanne and Vicki asked me why there wasn't a location manager.

Joanne was none too happy that the art department budget was equal to the wardrobe budget ($4000). I figured, in my infinite ignorance, that we could just find locations that would pretty much be in the condition we desired. Wrong. As for wardrobe, I knew Peter Gallagher would need four really nice suits, and then we had Ann, Cynthia, etc. John Hardy and I will try to find some money for Joanne, although she is valiantly trying to get us stuff for free from places she gave business to on *Everybody's All-American.*

Walt is becoming my personal hero. He offers to do (and then does) whatever has to be done in any area. Alex has shown herself to be incredibly resourceful, and so she was drafted to be 2nd A.D. John Hardy found a highly recommended A.D., Michael Dempsey, who is willing to come in on short notice from Texas for the paltry sum we've offered, so John and I are breathing much easier. We'll probably pay for Mike out of the contingency, although we've already saved some money in a few areas (locations, ironically).

The actors have arrived, and rehearsals start on Monday. The general consensus amongst those I know and trust is that the Graham backstory involving the retarded child is easily the dumbest subplot ever concocted for a minor motion picture, and I must say I am in agreement. I will go back to the more straightforward yet vague approach that I was using unsuccessfully before. I'll be rewriting during rehearsal anyway, so maybe somebody will come up with something better.

Aaron, Alex, and I found an apartment. It's pretty low-rent (which is the whole point of this production), but certainly serviceable. The cast and out-of-town crew members are staying at the Residence Inn, which is a really great place. I wish I could stay there.

We're shooting Agfa stock (high speed) instead of Kodak, because right now the Agfa high speed has more latitude, especially on the low end, and Walt and I may be going for some heavy contrast at certain points. We decided on a lab in Dallas, Allied+WBS, even though they haven't done much feature work. They have worked with Agfa, and they're very enthusiastic. It's often the case that when you go with a smaller company they really deliver the goods, because they're trying to establish themselves.

25–31 JUL 88

Rehearsals. Monday we (myself, Jimmy, Andie, Peter, Laura, and Ron) all sat around and did two read-throughs of the entire script. For the remainder of the week I broke everyone up into pairs (except for the dinner sequence, which has three characters). I kept my ears open for lines that sounded wrong or awkward. The only real improvising was between Jimmy and Laura, where the two of them essentially filled in what happens between the time when Cynthia is giving her penis speech and when she eventually takes her skirt off. It was truly fascinating to watch. I'd say they improvised for thirty minutes or so, Jimmy just circling, circling, cautious but still probing, and Laura bold but gradually revealing her vulnerability. They obviously have a very firm grasp of their characters. I'm glad somebody does.

The biggest issue during the week was (and is) what exactly should happen between Ann and Graham during the climactic taping scene after they've stopped talking. First of all, from the point where Ann picks up the camera to where they make physical contact still doesn't work dialogue-wise. And beyond that, how far should they go physically? How far do they have to go to satisfy themselves (and the audience)? I considered briefly having Ann on top of Graham and kind of dry-humping him to some sort of climax, but I chalked it up to having eaten too much Domino's pizza. It would be too quick a cure, and frankly I don't think I could ask that of Jimmy and Andie even if I didn't think it was a stupid idea. Jimmy is anxious to know what will happen so that he will have an idea of what he is leading up to. I'm stumped. We shoot Graham's apartment the last two weeks, so I've got three weeks to mess with it, but it's kind of scary not having it nailed right now.

Peter came up with some great stuff to loosen up John a little bit. He and I spent some time talking about his character while shooting targets with a plastic gun in his room. We got him some cool suits from Gilhe's (he's buying them when the film is done. Keith, at Gilhe's, is amazing with clothes. I've bought three suits and a tuxedo from him. Walking out, Peter said to me "That guy is an artist").

Some minor changes came about because of what is called a deForrest report, which is where some lawyers go through your script and basically tell you what you have to change in order to get an Errors and Omissions policy, which, of course, the bond company and RCA/Columbia require. John Moreau becomes John Millaney. The name of John's law firm is a problem. Every time I called to check on a new set of names, I was told one or more of the names were unacceptable. I'm blowing that off for now, since it's an offscreen voice. Looks like I'll have to forget about the Anais Nin diary. Just as well; people would read something into it, and I didn't mean anything by putting it there. I have to lose any reference to a power or utility company, since there are only two in Baton Rouge, and I can't imply that their employees would give out information!! A line of John's: "This conversation is loony tunes" provoked this response: "Reference to protected cartoon series of Warner Bros. Advise change." The one funny note was that there apparently *is* a Larry Carlson who works for IBM, so I changed the name to Brian Kirkland. I can't imagine what the deForrest report for *All the President's Men* looked like.

On Saturday we had a production meeting, and I gave a little speech to the whole crew. I'm really psyched about the film. At the very least, I know I'll enjoy making it, which is worth something.

During the week I bought an 8mm video camera and sent it to New York, where Jennifer Jason Leigh will attempt to record a cameo appearance as the "Girl on Tape." She and her boyfriend know Jimmy, and they offered to give it a try. I think it would be great if it happened. She seemed very nice the couple of times I talked to her, and Deb Aquila likes her very much (Deb just put the cast together for *Last Exit to Brooklyn,* in which Jennifer is playing the lead).

I got a call from Pat Dollard saying that Leading Artists was curious about my plans for representation. I told him that I couldn't replace Ann, and that unless he wanted to represent me, I would go without an agent. He called back a while later to say that was okay with everyone, and that actually some other clients of Ann's had requested the same thing. So Pat will be my agent. I'm glad it worked out this way.

I had fun hanging out late at the office and doing touch-up work on the script. At some level, I'm so happy this is happening that I want to soak up as much as I can, I guess.

I heard it was bad luck to start a shoot on a Monday. Fug dat shit.

"s e x ,   l i e s ,   a n d   v i d e o t a p e "

Leading Artists
445 N. Bedford Dr.
Penthouse
Beverly Hills, CA. 90210
213-858-1999

screenplay by
steven soderbergh
fourth draft
29 july 88
copyright 1988

1   EXT. HIGHWAY -- DAY   1

GRAHAM DALTON, twenty-nine, drives his ´69 Cutlass while smoking
a cigarette. One could describe his appearance as punk/arty,
but neither would do him justice. He is a man of obvious
intelligence, and his face is amiable. There is only one key
on his keyring, and it is in the ignition.

                    ANN
                  (voice over)
          Garbage. I started thinking about
          what happens to all the garbage.
          I mean, where do we put all of
          it, we have to run out of places
          to put it eventually, don´t we?
          This happened to me before when
          that barge with all the garbage
          was stranded and nobody would take
          it? Remember that?

2   INT. DOCTOR´S OFFICE -- DAY   2

ANN BISHOP MILLANEY, twenty-six, sits opposite her therapist.
She is an extremely attractive woman, dressed in a mature preppy
style. There is a wedding ring on her left hand.

                    DOCTOR
          Yes, I remember. What do you do
          when these moods overtake you?

                    ANN
          Nothing. I mean, <u>nothing</u>. I try
          not to do anything that will
          produce garbage, so obviously we´re
          talking about eating and basic
          stuff like that. Did you know that
          the average person produces three
          pounds of garbage a day?

                    DOCTOR
          No, I didn´t.

                    ANN
          Don´t you think that´s a lot of
          garbage? I´d really like to know
          where it´s all going to go.

                    DOCTOR
          Do you have any idea what triggered
          this concern?

                              (CONTINUED)

2   (CONTINUED)   2

>   ANN
> Well, this weekend John was taking
> out the garbage, and he kept
> spilling things out of the
> container, and I started imagining
> a container that grew garbage,
> like it just kept filling up and
> overflowing all by itself, and
> how could you stop that if it
> started happening?

>   DOCTOR
> Ann, do you see a pattern here?

>   ANN
> What do you mean?

>   DOCTOR
> Well, last week we talked about
> your obsession with the families
> of airline fatalities, and now
> we´re talking about your concern
> over the garbage problem.

>   ANN
> Yeah, so?

>   DOCTOR
> If you think about it, I think
> you´ll see that the object of your
> obsession is invariably something
> negative that you couldn´t possibly
> have any control over.

>   ANN
> Well, do you think many people
> run around thinking about how happy
> they feel and how great things
> are? I mean, maybe they do, but
> I doubt those people are in
> therapy. Besides, being happy isn´t
> all that great. My figure is always
> at its best when I´m depressed.
> The last time I was really happy
> I put on twenty-five pounds. I
> thought John was going to have
> a stroke.

>   JOHN
>   (voice over)
> It´s true, I´m telling you.

3   INT. LAW OFFICE -- DAY   3

JOHN MILLANEY, twenty-nine, sits at his desk talking on the
telephone. He is dressed very well, sporting real suspenders
with his striped pinpoint oxford shirt and cotton suit. He
fingers the wedding ring on his left hand.

> JOHN
> As soon as you´ve got a ring on
> your finger, you start getting
> serious attention from the opposite
> gender. Seriously, I wish I had
> Super Bowl seats for every time
> I had some philly just come up
> and start talking to me without
> the slightest provocation. That
> never happened before I got
> married. Shit, if I´d known that,
> I´d have gone out and bought me
> a ring when I was eighteen and
> saved myself a lot of time and
> money.

John looks at his watch.

> JOHN
> Shit, I gotta be someplace.
> (quickly)
> Look, racquetball Thursday? You´re
> the coolest.

John presses the intercom button while putting on his jacket.

> JOHN
> Uh, Janet, re-schedule Kirkland.
> Tell him to come in Friday at 1:30.

> DOCTOR
> (voice over, to Ann)
> Are you still keeping these
> thoughts from John?

> ANN
> (voice over)
> Yes.

4   INT. LAW OFFICE BATHROOM -- DAY   4

John brushes his teeth and combs his hair very carefully.

                                               (CONTINUED)

4   (CONTINUED)   4

                          DOCTOR
                    (voice over, to Ann)
               Are you afraid of his reaction?
               Of his finding you silly for
               thinking of such things?

                          ANN
                    (voice over)
               No. I don't know. I haven't told
               him about the garbage thing because
               I'm pissed off at him right now.
               He's letting some old college buddy
               stay at our house for a couple
               of days, and he didn't even ask
               me about it. I mean, I would've
               said yes, I just wish he would've
               asked.

5   INT. DOCTOR'S OFFICE -- DAY   5

                          DOCTOR
               What upsets you about that?

                          ANN
               I guess I'm upset because I can't
               really justify being upset, I mean,
               it's <u>his</u> house, really, <u>he</u> pays
               the mortgage.

                          DOCTOR
               But he asked you to quit your job,
               and you do have housework.

                          ANN
               Yeah, I know.

                          DOCTOR
               This unexpected visit
               notwithstanding, how are things
               with John?

                          ANN
                    (shrugs)
               Fine, I guess. Except right now
               I'm going through this where I
               don't want him to touch me.

6   INT. CYNTHIA BISHOP´S APARTMENT -- DAY   6

CYNTHIA BISHOP, Ann´s SISTER, opens her door to reveal the
freshly coiffed John Millaney. They kiss passionately and begin
to disrobe. Cynthia bears a slight resemblance to Ann, but
is not as overtly attractive. She does, however, have a definite
carnal appeal and air of confidence that Ann lacks.

                     DOCTOR
                 (voice over)
         When did you begin having this
         feeling?

                     ANN
                 (voice over)
         About a week ago. I don´t know
         what brought it on, I just started
         feeling like I didn´t want him
         to touch me.

                     DOCTOR
                 (voice over, to Ann)
         Prior to this feeling, were you
         comfortable having physical contact
         with him?

                     ANN
                 (voice over)
         Oh, yeah.
                 (pause)
         But see, I´ve never really been
         into sex that much, I mean, I <u>like</u>
         it and everything, it just doesn´t
         freak me out, I wouldn´t <u>miss</u> it,
         you know? But anyway, lately we
         haven´t been doing anything at
         all. Like I said, it´s not that
         I miss it, but I´m curious the
         way things kind of slacked off
         all of a sudden.

John and Cynthia are now having sex.

                     DOCTOR
                 (voice over)
         Perhaps he senses your hesitance
         at being touched.

                     ANN
                 (voice over)
         But see, he stopped <u>before</u> I got
         that feeling, that´s why it seems
         weird to me.
                 (more)

                         (CONTINUED)

6   (CONTINUED)   6

                         ANN (Cont´d)
          I mean, I´m sure he wishes I would
          initiate things once in awhile,
          and I would except it never occurs
          to me, I´m always thinking about
          something else and then the few
          times that I have felt like
          starting something I was by myself.

                         DOCTOR
                      (voice over)
          Did you do anything?

A pause.

                         ANN
                      (voice over)
          What do you mean?

                         DOCTOR
                      (voice over)
          Did you masturbate?

7   INT. DOCTOR´S OFFICE -- DAY   7

                         ANN
                      (taken aback)
          God, no.

                         DOCTOR
          I take it you´ve never masturbated?

                         ANN
                      (slightly uncomfortable)
          Well, I kind of tried once. It
          just seemed stupid, I kept seeing
          myself lying there and it seemed
          stupid, and kind of, uh, I don´t
          know, and then I was wondering
          if my dead grandfather could see
          me doing this, and it just seemed
          like a dumb thing to be doing when
          we don´t know what to do with all
          that garbage, you know?

                         DOCTOR
          So it was recently that you tried
          this.

                                        (CONTINUED)

7   (CONTINUED)   7

                  ANN
             (exhales, head down)
       Well, kind of recently, I guess.
       But not too recently.

There is a pause.

                  ANN
       I´m really not up to having a guest
       in the house.

8   INT. CYNTHIA BISHOP´S APARTMENT -- DAY   8

John and Cynthia are lying in bed, bathed in sweat.

                  JOHN
       I´ve got to get back to the office.

                  CYNTHIA
       I only get one today? Gee, how
       exciting.

John rolls over and begins to put his clothes on.

                  JOHN
       I can´t let my lunch hour go on
       too long. I´ve already skipped
       one meeting.

                  CYNTHIA
       Don´t give me this
       passive/aggressive bullshit. If
       you want to leave, <u>leave</u>. My life
       doesn´t stop when you walk out
       the door, you know what I´m saying?

John shakes his head.

                  JOHN
       Why don´t you just tell me how
       you <u>really</u> feel?

John stands and begins putting on his clothes.

                  JOHN
       I have a friend coming in from
       out of town, I´ll probably be
       spending some time with him the
       next couple of days.

                          (CONTINUED)

"sex, lies, and videotape"   pg.8

8   (CONTINUED)   8

                         CYNTHIA
               Meaning we´ll have to cool it for
               awhile, right?

                         JOHN
               Right.

A silent shrug from Cynthia. John is almost completely dressed.

                         JOHN
               I wish you´d quit that bartending
               job.

                         CYNTHIA
               Why?

                         JOHN
               I hate the thought of guys hitting
               on you all the time.

                         CYNTHIA
               I can handle it. Besides, the money
               is good and some of the guys are
               cute. And you are in no position
               to be jealous.

                         JOHN
               Who said I was jealous?

                         CYNTHIA
               I did.

John says nothing.

                         CYNTHIA
               You know, I´d like to try your
               house sometime. The idea of doing
               it in my sister´s bed gives me
               a perverse thrill.

John thinks about that.

                         CYNTHIA
               I wish I could tell everybody that
               Ann´s a lousy lay. Beautiful,
               popular, Ann Bishop Millaney.

                         JOHN
               Could be risky.

                                        (CONTINUED)

8   (CONTINUED) (2)   8

                              CYNTHIA
               Well, maybe I could just start
               a rumor, then.

                              JOHN
               No, I mean doing it at my house.

                              CYNTHIA
               Afraid of getting caught?

                              JOHN
               Maybe.

                              CYNTHIA
               You should be. Can I meet this
               friend of yours?

                              JOHN
               Cynthia, I don't think you want
               to, I mean, you should see the
               way he dresses. I really think
               he's in a bad way.

                              CYNTHIA
               I'm intrigued.

                              JOHN
               You're intrigued?

                              CYNTHIA
               Sure. Maybe he's the man I'm
               looking for. Then I won't have
               to fuck worried husbands all the
               time.

     John looks at her for a moment before heading for the door.

                              JOHN
               Bye.

9   EXT. JOHN AND ANN MILLANEY'S HOUSE -- DAY   9

     Graham has parked in the Millaney's driveway. He opens the
     trunk, revealing a Sony 8mm Video rig and a single black duffle
     bag. He grabs the duffle bag and shuts the trunk.

     Graham knocks at the door. He is stubbing out a cigarette with
     his beaten tennis shoe when Ann answers the door. She is unable
     to hide her suprise at his appearance.

                                          (CONTINUED)

"sex, lies, and videotape" pg.10

9 (CONTINUED) 9

>   GRAHAM
> Ann?

>   ANN
> Yes?

>   GRAHAM
>   (extends his hand)
> Graham Dalton.

Ann shakes his hand.

>   GRAHAM
> Can I use your bathroom?

Ann withdraws her hand.

>   ANN
> Yes. Yes, come in, please.

Graham moves inside.

10 INT. JOHN AND ANN MILLANEY'S HOUSE -- DAY   10

Ann closes the door and motions Graham to the rear of the house.

>   ANN
> Straight back, first door on the
> left.

Graham heads for the bathroom. Ann heads for the phone. She
dials John's office.

>   VOICE ON PHONE
> Forman, Brent, and Millaney.

>   ANN
> John Millaney, please. This is
> his wife.

Graham exits the bathroom. Ann quickly hangs up the phone.

>   ANN
> That was quick.

>   GRAHAM
> False alarm.

>   ANN
> Oh. Well, please sit down.

>   (CONTINUED)

10   (CONTINUED)   10

Graham sits, his manner pleasantly animated. He gets his Gitanes
from inside his scuffed black leather jacket and looks around
for an ashtray. Ann swallows uncomfortably.

                    ANN
          We...don´t usually let people smoke
          in the house. We have a patio if
          you--

                    GRAHAM
          Oh, no problem. It can wait.

A moment of silence. Graham looks at Ann directly. It is not
a challenging stare, he´s just trying to ascertain what kind
of person she is. Ann, to her credit, somehow meets his gaze.
Something subtle passes between them.

                    ANN
               (looks at duffle bag)
          Do you have other things?

                    GRAHAM
          Yes.
               (pause)
          Oh, you mean to bring in! No. Yes,
          I have some other things, no, I
          don´t need to bring them in. This
          is all I need to stay here.

                    ANN
          Oh.

Graham smiles. He has an unusual face, a face that flucuates
between remarkably handsome and just plain strange.

                    GRAHAM
          Have you ever been on television?

                    ANN
          Televison?

                    GRAHAM
          Yes.

                    ANN
          No. Why?

                    GRAHAM
               (shrugs)
          Curious.

The central air-conditioning switches on. Ann smiles.

                              (CONTINUED)

"sex, lies, and videotape"   pg.12

10   (CONTINUED) (2)   10

                         ANN
          Graham is an unusual name.

                         GRAHAM
          Yeah, I guess it is. My mother
          is a complete Anglophile, anything
          British makes her drool like a
          baby. She probably heard the name
          in some movie. She's a prisoner
          of public television now.

                         ANN
          Oh, uh-huh.

                         GRAHAM
          Are you uncomfortable with my
          appearance?

                         ANN
               (downplaying)
          No, I think you look...fine.

                         GRAHAM
               (smiles)
          Oh. Well, maybe I'm uncomfortable
          with my appearance. I feel a little
          out of place in these surroundings.

                         ANN
          Well...

                         GRAHAM
          I used to take great pleasure in
          that, being purposefully different,
          rubbing people's noses in it.
          Didn't you do that when you were
          younger?

                         ANN
               (thinks)
          No, not really.

                         GRAHAM
          Oh. Well, I did. I was in a band
          once, and the music was always
          secondary to just flat out
          offending as many people as
          possible.

                         ANN
          You play an instrument?

                                   (CONTINUED)

10　(CONTINUED) (3)　　　　　　　　　　　　　　10

> GRAHAM
> No, I was in charge of kind of
> standing at the microphone and
> reciting these really depressing
> lyrics in a monotone. The whole
> thing was really....irrelevent.
> How do you like being married?

> ANN
> (caught slightly off
> guard)
> Oh, I like it. I like it very much.

> GRAHAM
> What about it do you like? I´m
> not being critical, I´d really
> like to know.

> ANN
> Well.....well, the cliche about
> the security of it, that´s really
> true. We own a house, and I really
> like that, you know? And I like
> that John was just made junior
> partner, so he has a steady job
> and he´s not some...

Ann looks at Graham and stops. He smiles again.

> ANN
> ...free-lance. You know.

> GRAHAM
> Yes. So you feel security,
> stability. Like things are going
> to last awhile.

> ANN
> Oh, definitely. I mean, just this
> past year has gone by like phew!
> I hardly even knew it passed.

> GRAHAM
> Did you know that if you shut
> someone up in a room, and the only
> clock he has reference to runs
> two hours slow for every
> twenty-four, that his body will
> eventually adjust to that schedule?
> Simply because the mind honestly
> perceives that twenty-six hours
> are twenty-four, the body follows.

> (CONTINUED)

10   (CONTINUED)   (4)   10

                          GRAHAM
                                    And
          then there are sections of time.
          Your life can be broken down into
          the sections of time that formed
          your personality (if you have one).
          For instance, when I was twelve,
          I had an eleven minute conversation
          with my father that to this day
          defines our relationship. Now,
          I´m not saying that everything
          happened in that specific section
          of time, but the events of my
          childhood involving my father led
          up to, and then were crystallized
          in, that eleven minutes.

Ann is fascinated, if a bit overwhelmed.

                          ANN
          Oh, uh-huh.

                          GRAHAM
                    (smiles)
          Anyway, I think the mind is very
          flexible as far as time is
          concerned.

                          ANN
          You mean like "time flies"?

                          GRAHAM
          Exactly. I would say the fact that
          you feel the first year of your
          marriage has gone by quickly means
          lots of things. Or could mean lots
          of things.

                          ANN
          How long has it been since you´ve
          seen John?

                          GRAHAM
          Nine years.

                          ANN
          Nine years?

                                        (CONTINUED)

10   (CONTINUED) (5)   10

                         GRAHAM
                Yes. I was surprised that he
                accepted when I asked if I could
                stay here until I found a place.

                         ANN
                Why? Didn´t you know him well?

                         GRAHAM
                I knew him <u>very</u> well. We were
                extremely close until I dropped
                out.

A pause.

                         ANN
                Why´d you drop out?

                         GRAHAM
                Oh, lots of reasons, most of them
                boring. But, up until I dropped
                out, John and I were...very much
                alike.

                         ANN
                That´s hard to believe. The two
                of you seem so different.

                         GRAHAM
                I would imagine that we are, now.
                I think I´m ready to use the
                bathroom, finally.

Graham gets up and heads for the toilet. Ann watches him go,
a bemused smile on her face. After she hears the door close,,
she can´t resist the impulse to take a closer look at Graham´s
bag.

IN THE BATHROOM, Graham pokes around, looking through the
medicine cabinet and sniffing towels.

                         JOHN
                    (voice over)
                Call the cops.

11   INT. JOHN AND ANN MILLANEY´S HOUSE -- NIGHT   11

John, Ann and Graham are eating dinner.

                                        (CONTINUED)

11   (CONTINUED)   11

> JOHN
> (to Graham)
> That´s the first thing that ran
> through my mind when I saw you.
> I thought this is not the same
> man that rode the unicycle naked
> through the homecoming parade.

> ANN
> (to Graham)
> You did that?

> GRAHAM
> Everybody has a past.

> JOHN
> (smiles at Graham)
> What do you think the Greeks would
> make of that outfit you´re wearing?

> GRAHAM
> A bonfire, probably.

John takes a sip of Chivas.

> GRAHAM
> (to Ann)
> This food is excellent.

> ANN
> Thank you.

> JOHN
> Yeah, it´s not bad. Usually Ann
> has some serious salt action going.
> I keep telling her, you can always
> add more if you want, but you can´t
> take it out.

> GRAHAM
> (to Ann)
> You have family here also?

> ANN
> (nods, chewing)
> Mother, father, sister.

> GRAHAM
> Sister older or younger?

> ANN
> Younger.

(CONTINUED)

11   (CONTINUED) (2)   11

John takes a large swig of Chivas.

>   GRAHAM
>   Are you close?

Graham sees Ann and John exchange looks.

>   GRAHAM
>   I´m sorry. Am I prying again?

>   JOHN
>   You were prying before?

>   GRAHAM
>   Yes, this afternoon. I was grilling
>   Ann about your marriage this
>   afternoon.

>   JOHN
>   (smiles)
>   Really. How´d it go?

>   GRAHAM
>   She held up very well.

Ann laughs.

>   GRAHAM
>   (to Ann)
>   So I was asking about your sister.

Ann´s smile fades. John resumes eating.

>   ANN
>   Oh, we get along okay. She´s just
>   very...she´s an extrovert. I think
>   she´s loud. She probably wouldn´t
>   agree. <u>Definitely</u> wouldn´t agree.

>   JOHN
>   (to Graham)
>   Are you going to see Elizabeth
>   while you´re here?

An almost imperceptible reaction by Graham.

>   GRAHAM
>   I don´t know.

>   ANN
>   (interested)
>   Who´s Elizabeth?

(CONTINUED)

11   (CONTINUED)   (3)   11

                         JOHN
               Girl Graham dated. Still lives
               here, far as I know.

Graham eats in silence.

                         ANN
               Graham and I were talking about
               apartments and I told him to check
               the Garden District, there are
               some nice little places there,
               garage apartments and stuff.

                         JOHN
                    (to Graham)
               Stay away from the Garden District.
               Serious crime. I don´t know what
               kind of place you´re looking for,
               but there are a lot of studio-type
               apartments available elsewhere.

                         GRAHAM
               I wish I didn´t have to live
               someplace.

                         JOHN
                    (laughs)
               What do you mean?

Graham thinks a moment, then puts his keyring with its single
key onto the table.

                         GRAHAM
               Well, see, right now I have this
               one key, and I really like that.
               Everything I own is in my car.
               If I get an apartment, that´s two
               keys. If I get a job, maybe I
               have to open and close once in
               awhile, that´s more keys. Or I
               buy some stuff and I´m worried
               about getting ripped off, so I
               get some locks, and that´s more
               keys. I just really like having
               the one key. It´s clean, you know?

Graham looks at the keyring before returning it to his pocket.

                         JOHN
               Get rid of the car when you get
               your apartment, then you´ll still
               have one key.

                                        (CONTINUED)

11   (CONTINUED) (4)   11

> GRAHAM
> I like having the car, the car
> is important.

> JOHN
> Especially if you want to leave
> someplace in a hurry.

> GRAHAM
> Or go someplace in a hurry.

Ann takes her plate into the kitchen.

> JOHN
> (smiles at Graham)
> Do you pay taxes?

Graham also stands, empty plate in hand.

> GRAHAM
> Do I pay taxes? Of course I pay
> taxes, only a liar doesn´t pay
> taxes, I´m not a liar. A liar is
> the second lowest form of human
> being.

> ANN
> (from the kitchen)
> What´s the first?

> GRAHAM
> Lawyers.

John smiles, thinking. Graham follows Ann into the kitchen.
John shouts after them.

> JOHN
> Hey, Ann, why don´t you go with
> Graham to hunt for apartments?
> Show him how the city has changed.

Ann looks at Graham.

> ANN
> Would you mind?

> GRAHAM
> No.

> ANN
> (shouts back to John)
> Okay, I will!!

(CONTINUED)

"sex, lies, and videotape" pg.20

11 (CONTINUED) (5) 11

John, sitting at the table and now toying with <u>his</u> keyring, nods.

12 INT. JOHN AND ANN MILLANEY'S HOUSE -- NIGHT 12

Everyone but Ann is asleep. She gets up from her bed and sneaks quietly into the guest bedroom where Graham is staying. She walks cautiously up to his bed to watch him as he sleeps. Moonlight caresses his face as he breathes peacefully. Exhaling, he turns over slowly, his back to Ann.

She picks up his jacket from beside the bed and feels the surface. She brings the jacket to her nose, inhaling his presence. She then sets the jacket down.

13 INT. CYNTHIA BISHOP'S APARTMENT -- DAY 13

The phone rings. Cynthia answers.

> CYNTHIA
> Hello.

> JOHN
> Cynthia. John. Meet me at my house
> in exactly one hour.

> CYNTHIA
> You are scum. I'll be there.

14 INT. VACANT APARTMENT -- DAY 14

Graham and Ann walk around the room, their footfalls heavy on the hardwood floors. MR. MILLER, the landlord, stands nearby. He looks fairly interested in Ann.

> MR. MILLER
> Plenty of room for two people.

> GRAHAM
> It'll just be me.

> MR. MILLER
> Student?

> GRAHAM
> No.
>   (pause)
> You said three-fifty?

(CONTINUED)

14   (CONTINUED)   14

                      MR. MILLER
        Plus first and last month deposit.

                      GRAHAM
        Will you lease month-to-month?

                      MR. MILLER
        Not for three-fifty.

                      GRAHAM
        How about for five hundred?

Mr. Miller looks at Ann, then back at Graham.

                      MR. MILLER
        That I can do.

15   INT. JOHN AND ANN MOREAU'S HOUSE -- DAY   15

Cynthia lets herself in. She looks around.

                      CYNTHIA
        John?

                      JOHN
                  (offscreen)
        In here!!

Cynthia walks to the bedroom, where John lies naked on the bed.
She smiles, kicking off her shoes.

                      CYNTHIA
        Ain't you a picture.

Cynthia begins taking her clothes off. She places her diamond
stud earring in her jacket pocket, and then drops the jacket
on the floor. She moves onto the bed with John.

                      ANN
                  (voice over)
        Maybe you'll understand this,
        because you know John, but he
        confuses me sometimes.

                      GRAHAM
                  (voice over)
        How do you mean?

16   INT. CAFE -- DAY   16

Graham and Ann are having lunch. Ann looks to have had a lot
of wine. Graham drinks club soda with a twist.

                    ANN
          It's hard to explain. It's like...
          John treats everybody the <u>same</u>,
          you know? I mean, he acts <u>just</u>
          as excited about seeing somebody
          he hardly knows as he does when
          he sees me. And so I feel like,
          what's different about me, if I'm
          treated <u>exactly</u> the same as some
          acquaintance? If I don't like
          somebody, I don't act like I do.
          I guess that's why a lot of people
          think I'm a bitch.

She takes a sip of wine.

                    GRAHAM
          Yeah, I know. I mean, I'm not
          saying I know people think you're
          a bitch, I'm saying I know what
          you mean. And I don't even know
          that people think you're a bitch.
          Do they?

                    ANN
          I feel like they do.

                    GRAHAM
          Hmm. Well, maybe you are. Really,
          I wouldn't pay much attention.

Ann smiles.

                    GRAHAM
          I know that I just don't feel a
          <u>connection</u> with very many people,
          so I don't waste time with people
          I don't feel one with.

                    ANN
          Right, right. I don't feel
          connected to many people, either.
          Other than John.

Graham nods.

                              (CONTINUED)

16   (CONTINUED)   16

                     ANN
Can I tell you something personal?
I feel like I can. It's something
I couldn't tell John. Or <u>wouldn't</u>,
anyway.

                   GRAHAM
It's up to you. But I warn you,
if you tell me something personal,
I might do the same.

                     ANN
Okay. I <u>think</u>...I think sex is
overrated. I think people place
way too much importance on it.
And I think that stuff about women
wanting it just as bad is crap.
I'm not saying women don't want
it, I just don't think they want
it for the reason men <u>think</u> they
do.
    (smiles)
I'm getting confused.

Graham smiles.

                     ANN
Do you understand what I'm trying
to say?

                   GRAHAM
I think so. I remember reading
somewhere that men learn to love
what they're attracted to, whereas
women become more and more
attracted to the person they love.

                     ANN
Yes! Yes! I think that's very true.
Very.

Graham watches Ann take a sip of wine.

                   GRAHAM
So what about kids?

                     ANN
Kids? What about them?

                   GRAHAM
Do you want them?

                              (CONTINUED)

16   (CONTINUED) (2)   16

                         ANN
               Yeah, actually, I do. But John
               doesn't. At least not right now.

                         GRAHAM
               Why is that?

                         ANN
               I don't know, he just said he wants
               to wait. I quit asking.

Graham nods.

                         ANN
               So what's your personal thing?
               Are you really going to tell me
               something personal?

                         GRAHAM
               Do you want me to?

                         ANN
               As long as it's not...<u>gross</u>, you
               know? Like some scar or something.
               It has to be like mine, like
               something <u>about</u> you.

                         GRAHAM
               Agreed.

Graham takes a sip of club soda.

                         GRAHAM
               I'm impotent.

Ann looks at him closely.

                         ANN
               You're <u>what</u>?

                         GRAHAM
               Impotent.

                         ANN
               You <u>are</u>?

                         GRAHAM
               Well, let me put it this way: I
               cannot achieve an erection while
               in the presence of another person.
               So, for all practical purposes,
               I am impotent.

                                        (CONTINUED)

"sex, lies, and videotape"   pg.25

16   (CONTINUED) (3)   16

Ann takes a large sip of wine. Graham lights a cigarette.

           ANN
Does it bother you?

           GRAHAM
           (exhales)
Not usually. I mean, honestly,
I haven't known many guys that
could think straight with an
erection, so I feel I'm way ahead
of the game as far as being
clear-headed goes.

           ANN
Well...are you self-conscious about
it?

           GRAHAM
I am self-conscious, but not in
the same way that you are. You
have got to be the most attractive
self-conscious person I've ever
seen.

           ANN
Why do you say I'm self-conscious?

           GRAHAM
Well, I've been watching you. I've
watched you eat, I've watched you
speak, I've watched the way you
<u>move</u>, and I see somebody who is
extremely conscious of being looked
at. I think you really believe
that people are looking at you
all the time. And you know what?

           ANN
What?

           GRAHAM
They <u>are</u> looking at you. Ann, you
are truly breathtaking. I don't
know if you understand how your
appearance can affect people. Men
want to possess you, women wish
they looked like you. And those
that don't or can't resent you.
And the fact that you're a nice
person just makes it worse.

                    (CONTINUED)

"sex, lies, and videotape"   pg.26

16   (CONTINUED)   (4)   16

                    ANN
                 (thinks)
          My therapist said that--

                    GRAHAM
          You´re in therapy?

                    ANN
          Aren´t you?

                    GRAHAM
          Hah! No, I´m not. Actually, I used
          to be, but the therapist I had
          was really ineffectual in helping
          me deal with my problems. Of
          course, I lied to him constantly,
          so I guess I can´t hold him totally
          responsible...

                    ANN
          So you don´t believe in therapy?

                    GRAHAM
          I believe in it for some people.
          I mean, for me it was silly, I
          was confused going in. So I just
          formed my own personal theory that
          you should never take advice from
          someone of the opposite sex that
          doesn´t know you intimately.

                    ANN
          Well, my therapist knows me
          intimately.

                    GRAHAM
                 (surprised)
          You had sex with you therapist?

                    ANN
          Of course not.

                    GRAHAM
          Oh, see, I meant someone you´ve
          had sex with. That´s part of the
          theory.

                    ANN
          Excuse me for asking, but how would
          you know?

                              (CONTINUED)

16   (CONTINUED) (5)   16

                          GRAHAM
                     (smiles)
                Well, I wasn´t <u>always</u> impotent.

Ann takes another sip of wine and thinks for a moment.

                          ANN
                Now, you said never take advice
                from someone that you don´t know
                intimately, right?

                          GRAHAM
                Basically, yes.

17   INT. JOHN AND ANN MILLANEY -- DAY   17

Cynthia is leaving the house. She gives John a big kiss.

                          ANN
                     (voice over)
                So since I´ve never had sex with
                you, by your own advice I shouldn´t
                accept your advice.

                          GRAHAM
                     (voice over)
                That´s correct.
                     (pause)
                Bit of a dilemma, isn´t it?

Cynthia is not wearing her diamond stud earring.

18   INT. DOCTOR´S OFFICE -- DAY   18

                          ANN
                Well, I don´t know. The week
                started off okay, but then I was
                outside watering the plants, and
                I started feeling dizzy from the
                heat and that got me thinking about
                the Greenhouse Effect, so I went
                inside and turned on the
                air-conditioner full blast, and
                that made me feel a little better
                until I started thinking about
                radon leakage coming up through
                the floor, and--

                          DOCTOR
                Radon leakage?

                                        (CONTINUED)

"sex, lies, and videotape"   pg.28

18   (CONTINUED)   18

                         ANN
          Yes, it's this radioactive gas
          in the ground, and houses kind
          of act like magnets to pull it
          up, and--you've never heard of
          this?

                       DOCTOR
          No, I haven't.

                         ANN
          Well, the cumulative effect is
          not good, let me tell you.
                    (pause)
          I knew I shouldn't have watered
          those plants.

                       DOCTOR
          Did you confront John about the
          visitor?

                         ANN
          What visitor?

                       DOCTOR
          The friend of John's that was
          staying at your house.

                         ANN
          Oh, Graham. No, I didn't talk to
          him about that. Actually, that
          turned out to be pretty
          interesting. I expected Graham
          to be this...well, like John, you
          know? I mean, he said they had
          gone to school together, so I was
          expecting lots of stories about
          getting drunk and secret handshakes
          and stuff. But he turned out to
          be this...this kind of character,
          I mean, he's kind of arty but okay,
          you know?

                       DOCTOR
          Is he still at your house?

                         ANN
          No, he left last week.

                       DOCTOR
          Did you find him attractive?

                              (CONTINUED)

18   (CONTINUED) (2)   18

                         ANN
          What do you mean, like physically?

                         DOCTOR
          Let me rephrase. Were you attracted
          <u>to</u> him?

                         ANN
                    (thinks)
          I guess, but not because of the
          way he looked or anything. He's
          just so <u>different</u>, somebody new
          to have a conversation with. I'm
          just tired of talking to other
          couples about whether or not
          they're going to buy the station
          wagon, you know? It's just <u>boring</u>.
          I don't know, he was just
          different. And he's really on about
          truth a lot, being honest, and
          I like that, I felt comfortable
          around him.
                    (pause)
          After he left I had a dream that
          he signed a lease to rent our guest
          room.

                         CYNTHIA
                    (voice over)
          So where's he from?

19   INT. CYNTHIA BISHOP'S APARTMENT -- DAY   19

      Ann stands watching Cynthia get dressed for work.

                         ANN
          I don't know. He went to school
          here, then he was in New York for
          awhile, then Philadelphia, and
          then just kind of travelling
          around.

                         CYNTHIA
          Must be nice. So, what's he like,
          is he like John?

                         ANN
          No, not at all. Actually, I don't
          think John likes him much anymore.
          He said he thought Graham had
          gotten strange.

                                        (CONTINUED)

"sex, lies, and videotape"   pg.30

19   (CONTINUED)   19

                         CYNTHIA
               Is he? Strange, I mean?

                         ANN
               Not really. Maybe if I just saw
               him on the street I´d have said
               that, but after talking to
               him...he´s just kind of...I don´t
               know, unusual.

                         CYNTHIA
               Uh-huh. So what´s he look like?

     A pause.

                         ANN
               Why?

                         CYNTHIA
               I just want to know what he looks
               like, is all.

                         ANN
               Why, so you can go after him?

                         CYNTHIA
               Jesus, Ann, get a life. I just
               asked what he looked like.

     Ann says nothing.

                         CYNTHIA
               Besides, even if I decided to fuck
               his brains out, what business is
               that of yours?

                         ANN
               Do you have to say that?

                         CYNTHIA
               What?

                         ANN
               You know what. You say it just
               to irritate me.

                         CYNTHIA
               I say it because it´s descriptive.

                                        (CONTINUED)

19   (CONTINUED) (2)   19

                         ANN
          Well, he doesn´t strike me as the
          kind of person that would go in
          for that sort of thing, anyway.

                    CYNTHIA
          Ann, you always underestimate me.

                         ANN
          Well, I wonder why.

                    CYNTHIA
          I think you´re afraid to put the
          two of us in the same room
          together. I think you´re afraid
          he´ll be undeniably <u>drawn</u> to me.

                         ANN
          Oh, for God´s sake. Really,
          Cynthia, really, I don´t think
          he´s your type.

                    CYNTHIA
          "My type"? What is this bullshit?
          How would you know what "my type"
          is?

                         ANN
          I have a pretty good idea.

                    CYNTHIA
          Ann, you don´t have a clue. Look,
          I don´t even know why we´re
          discussing this, I´ll just call
          him myself.

                         ANN
          He doesn´t have a phone.

                    CYNTHIA
          Well, I´ll call him when he does.

                         ANN
          But he won´t.

                    CYNTHIA
          What are you talking about?

                         ANN
          He´s not getting a phone, he
          doesn´t like talking on the phone.

                              (CONTINUED)

19   (CONTINUED) (3)   19

                         CYNTHIA
          Oh, <u>please</u>. Okay, so give me the
          Zen master's address, I'll think
          of a reason to stop by.

                         ANN
          Let me talk to him first.

                         CYNTHIA
          Why? Just give me the address,
          you won't even have to be involved.

                         ANN
          I don't feel right just <u>giving</u>
          you the address so that <u>you</u> can
          go over there and...

                         CYNTHIA
          And what?

                         ANN
          And...do whatever it is you do.

Cynthia laughs loudly. Ann, not happy, watches her dig through
the jewelry box.

                         ANN
          Lose something?

                         CUTNHIA
          That goddam diamond stud earring
          that cost me a fucking fortune.

                         ANN
          Are you getting Mom something for
          her birthday?

                         CYNTHIA
          I don't know, I'll get her a card
          or something.

                         ANN
          A <u>card</u>? For her fiftieth birthday?

                         CYNTHIA
          What's wrong with that?

                         ANN
          Don't you think she deserves a
          little more than a card? I mean,
          the woman gave birth to you. It's
          her fiftieth birthday--

                              (CONTINUED)

19   (CONTINUED) (4)   19

                    CYNTHIA
          Will you stop? Jesus.

                    ANN
          I just thought it might--

                    CYNTHIA
          Okay, <u>Ann</u>, okay. How about this:
          you buy her something nice, and
          I'll pay for half. All right?

                    ANN
          Fine.

                    CYNTHIA
          Good. Now, if you'll pardon me,
          <u>I</u> have to go to work.

20   INT. DOCTOR'S OFFICE -- DAY   20

                    ANN
          I was thinking maybe I shouldn't
          be in therapy anymore.

                    DOCTOR
          What brought this on?

                    ANN
          I've been thinking about it for
          awhile, and then I was talking
          to somebody who kind of put things
          in perspective for me.

                    DOCTOR
               (smiles)
          I thought that's what I did. Who
          was it that you talked to?

                    ANN
          That guy Graham I told you about.
          He said taking advice from someone
          you don't know intimately
          was...well, he said a lot of stuff.

The Doctor exhales, thinking for a moment.

                    DOCTOR
          Ann, in life one has to be aware
          of hidden agendas.
               (more)

                                        (CONTINUED)

20   (CONTINUED)   20

                   DOCTOR (Cont´d)
Did it occur to you that Graham
may have his own reasons for not
wanting you to be in therapy?

                   ANN
What do you mean? I don´t
understand.

                   DOCTOR
It´s possible that Graham has
hidden motives for disliking
therapy and/or therapists. Perhaps
he has problems of his own that
he is unwilling to deal with, and
he would like to see other people,
you for instance, wallow in their
situation just as he does. Do you
think that´s possible?

                   ANN
I guess.

                   DOCTOR
You understand that you <u>are</u> free
to leave therapy at any time?

                   ANN
Yes.

                   DOCTOR
That you are under no obligation
to me?

                   ANN
Yes.

                   DOCTOR
Do you want to leave therapy?

                   ANN
Not really.

                   DOCTOR
Do you feel there is more progress
to be made?

                   ANN
Yes.

                   (CONTINUED)

20   (CONTINUED) (2)   20

                              DOCTOR
              I'm glad you feel that way, because
              I feel that way, too.

                              ANN
              But you don't have hidden motives
              for feeling that way, right?

The Doctor laughs. Ann does not laugh with him.

21   INT. GRAHAM'S APARTMENT -- DAY   21

On a television monitor we see images originating from an 8mm
Video deck. Graham sits naked in a sheet-covered chair facing
the screen. He watches the tape, which is footage of himself
interviewing a girl about her sexual preferences. The
photography on the tape is handheld, relentless. As the
questions get more detailed, Graham becomes more aroused.

There is a knock on Graham's door. He calmly shuts off the
videotape player and stands, wrapping the sheet around himself.

                              GRAHAM
              It's open.

Graham walks into the bedroom to put on some clothes. Ann opens
the door and walks into the apartment.

                              ANN
              Hi!

                              GRAHAM
                     (off)
              Ann. Hello.

                              ANN
              Are you in the middle of something?

                              GRAHAM
                     (off)
              Nothing I can't finish later.

                              ANN
                     (looks)
              I just wanted to see how the place
              looked furnished.

                                        (CONTINUED)

"sex, lies, and videotape"   pg.36

21   (CONTINUED)   21

                         GRAHAM
                    (off)
               Not much to see, I´m afraid. I´m
               sort of cultivating a minimalist
               vibe.

                         ANN
               Somehow I imagined books. I thought
               you would have like a whole lot
               of books and be reading all the
               time.

Graham enters.

                         GRAHAM
               I do read a lot. But I check
               everything out of the library.

Graham picks up an Anais Nin diary and opens it to show Ann
the library sleeve inside.

                         GRAHAM
               Cheaper that way. And cuts down
               on the clutter.

Ann walks to the table where the video gear is set up. Graham
watches her closely. She looks into a large box of 8mm
videotapes. On the side of each tape is a label. The labels
look like this:

DONNA / 11 DEC 86 / 1:07:36

And so on. There are thirty or forty tapes, total.

                         ANN
               What are these?

                         GRAHAM
               Videotapes.

                         ANN
                    (smiles)
               I can <u>see</u> that. What are they?

Graham exhales.

                         GRAHAM
               It´s a personal project I´m working
               on.

                                        (CONTINUED)

21   (CONTINUED) (2)   21

>   ANN
>   What kind of personal project?
>
>   GRAHAM
>   Oh, just a personal project like
>   anyone else´s personal project.
>   Mine´s just a little more personal.
>
>   ANN
>   Who´s Donna?
>
>   Donna?   GRAHAM
>
>   ANN
>   Donna. On this tape it says
>   "Donna".
>
>   GRAHAM
>   (thinking)
>   Donna was a girl I knew in Florida.
>
>   ANN
>   You went out with her?
>
>   GRAHAM
>   Not really.

Ann looks in the box again.

>   ANN
>   How come all these are girl´s
>   names?

Graham thinks for a moment.

>   GRAHAM
>   Because I enjoy interviewing women
>   more than men.
>
>   ANN
>   All of these are interviews?
>
>   GRAHAM
>   Yes.
>
>   ANN
>   Can we look at one?
>
>   GRAHAM
>   No.

                                        (CONTINUED)

21   (CONTINUED) (3)   21

                          ANN
          Why not?

                          GRAHAM
          Because I promised each subject
          that no one would look at the tape
          except me.

Ann looks at Graham for a long moment, then back at the tapes.

                          ANN
          What...what are these interviews
          about?

                          GRAHAM
          The...interviews are about sex,
          Ann.

                          ANN
          About sex?

                          GRAHAM
          Yes.

                          ANN
          What about sex?

                          GRAHAM
          Everything about sex.

                          ANN
          Like what?

                          GRAHAM
          Like what they've done, what they
          do, what they don't do, what they
          want to do but are afraid to ask
          for, what they won't do even if
          asked. Anything I can think of.

                          ANN
          You just ask them questions?

                          GRAHAM
          Yes.

                          ANN
          And they just answer them?

                          GRAHAM
          Mostly. Sometimes they do things.

                                    (CONTINUED)

21   (CONTINUED) (4)   21

                    ANN
       To you?

                    GRAHAM
       No, not <u>to</u> me, <u>for</u> me, for the
       camera.

                    ANN
          (stunned)
       I don´t....why...why do you do
       this?

                    GRAHAM
       I´m sorry this came up.

                    ANN
       This is just....so...

                    GRAHAM
       Maybe you want to go.

                    ANN
       Yes, I do.

Ann nods and absently heads for the door. She gives Graham a
puzzled look before leaving.

22   INT. JOHN AND ANN MILLANEY´S HOUSE -- DAY   22

Ann is talking to Cynthia on the telephone.

                    ANN
          (still shaken)
       I don´t...he doesn´t want you to
       come over.

                    CYNTHIA
       What do you mean he doesn´t want
       me to come over? Did you tell him
       about me?

                    ANN
       No, I didn´t.

                    CYNTHIA
       Why not?

                    ANN
       Because I never got around to it.

                        (CONTINUED)

"sex, lies, and videotape"   pg.40

22   (CONTINUED)   22

                         CYNTHIA
               Well, why?

                         ANN
               Because. Cynthia, look, John was
               right. Graham <u>is</u> strange. Very
               strange. You don´t want to get
               involved with him.

                         CYNTHIA
               What the hell happened over there?
               Did he make a pass at you?

                         ANN
               No!

                         CYNTHIA
               Then what´s the story, what´s this
               "strange" bullshit all of a sudden?
               Is he drowning puppies, or what?

                         ANN
               No, it´s nothing like that.

                         CYNTHIA
               Well, what? Is he dangerous?

                         ANN
               No, he´s not dangerous. Not
               physically.

                         CYNTHIA
               Well, <u>what</u>, then?

                         ANN
               I don´t want to talk about it.

                         CYNTHIA
               Then why´d you call me?

                         ANN
               I don´t know.

     Ann hangs up.

23   INT. CYNTHIA BISHOP´S APARTMENT -- DAY   23

     Cynthia gets out of the shower. The phone rings. She wraps
     herself in a towel and lifts the receiver.

                                        (CONTINUED)

23   (CONTINUED)   23

                         CYNTHIA
            Hello.

                         JOHN
            Cynthia. John.

                         CYNTHIA
            Not today. I´ve got other plans.

                         JOHN
            Oh.
                 (pause)
            Well, <u>when</u>, then?

                         CYNTHIA
            How about inviting me over to
            dinner?

                         JOHN
            You know what I mean.

                         CYNTHIA
            Yeah, I know what you mean.

      Cynthia hangs up the phone.

24   INT. GRAHAM´S APARTMENT -- DAY   24

      Graham sits smoking a cigarette. There is a knock at his door.

                         GRAHAM
            It´s open.

      Cynthia enters. Graham looks up at her.

                         GRAHAM
            Who are you?

                         CYNTHIA
            I´m Cynthia Bishop.

                         GRAHAM
            Do I know you?

                         CYNTHIA
            I´m Ann Millaney´s sister.

                         GRAHAM
            The extrovert.

                                             (CONTINUED)

24   (CONTINUED)   24

                    CYNTHIA
                 (smiles)
          She must have been in a good mood
          when she said that. She usually
          calls me loud.

                    GRAHAM
          She called you that, too. May I
          ask why you're here?

                    CYNTHIA
          You want me to leave?

                    GRAHAM
          I just want to know why you're
          here.

                    CYNTHIA
          Well, like I said, Ann is my
          sister. Sisters talk. You can
          imagine the rest.

                    GRAHAM
          No, I really can't. I find it
          healthy never to characterize
          people I don't know or
          conversations I haven't heard.
          I don't know what you and your
          sister discussed about me or
          anything else. Last time I saw
          Ann she left here very...confused,
          I would say. And upset.

                    CYNTHIA
          She still is.

                    GRAHAM
          And are you here to berate me for
          making her that way?

                    CYNTHIA
          Nope.

                    GRAHAM
          She didn't tell you why she was
          upset?

                    CYNTHIA
          Nope.

                    GRAHAM
          She didn't give you my address?

                              (CONTINUED)

24   (CONTINUED) (2)   24

                         CYNTHIA
                    Nope.

                         GRAHAM
                    How did you find me?

                         CYNTHIA
                    I, uh, know a guy at the power
                    company.

                         GRAHAM
                    I don't understand. Why did you
                    want to come here? I mean, I can't
                    imagine Ann painted a very
                    flattering portrait of me.

                         CYNTHIA
                    Well, I don't really listen to
                    her when it comes to men. I mean,
                    look at John, for crissake. Oh,
                    you went to school with him didn't
                    you? You're probably friends or
                    something.

                         GRAHAM
                    Nope. I think the man is a liar.

                         CYNTHIA
                         (smiles)
                    I think you're right. So come on,
                    I came all the way over here to
                    find out what got Ann so spooked,
                    tell me what happened.

                         GRAHAM
                         (smiles)
                    Spooked.

He motions to the box of videotapes.

                         GRAHAM
                    That box of tapes is what got Ann
                    so "spooked".

Cynthia goes over to the box and looks inside for a long moment,
studying the labels.

                         CYNTHIA
                    Oh, okay. I think I get it.

                         GRAHAM
                    What do you get?

                                              (CONTINUED)

"sex, lies, and videotape"   pg.44

24   (CONTINUED) (3)   24

                    CYNTHIA
Well, they must be something
sexual, because Ann gets freaked
out by that shit. Are these tapes
of you having sex with these girls
or something?

                    GRAHAM
Not exactly.

                    CYNTHIA
Well, either you are or you aren´t.
Which is it?

                    GRAHAM
Why don´t you let me tape you?

                    CYNTHIA
Doing what?

                    GRAHAM
Talking.

                    CYNTHIA
About what?

                    GRAHAM
Sex. Your sexual history, your
sexual preferences.

                    CYNTHIA
What makes you think I´d discuss
that with you?

                    GRAHAM
Nothing.

                    CYNTHIA
You just want to ask me questions?

                    GRAHAM
I just want to ask you questions.

                    CYNTHIA
And that´s all?

                    GRAHAM
That´s all.

                                        (CONTINUED)

24   (CONTINUED) (4)   24

                         CYNTHIA
                   (a crooked smile)
          Is this how you get off or
          something? Taping women talking
          about their sexual experiences?

                         GRAHAM
          Yes.

                         CYNTHIA
          Would anybody else see the tape?

                         GRAHAM
          Absolutely not. They are for my
          private use only.

                         CYNTHIA
          How do we start?

                         GRAHAM
          I turn on the camera. You start
          talking.

                         CYNTHIA
          And you ask questions, right?

                         GRAHAM
          Yes.

                         CYNTHIA
          How long will it take?

                         GRAHAM
          That depends on you. One woman
          only used three minutes. Another
          filled up three two hour tapes.

                         CYNTHIA
          Can I see some of the other tapes
          to get an idea of what--

                         GRAHAM
          No.

                         CYNTHIA
                   (thinks)
          Do I sit or stand?

                         GRAHAM
          Whichever you prefer.

                                        (CONTINUED)

24   (CONTINUED) (5)   24

>   CYNTHIA
>   I´d rather sit. Are you ready?

>   GRAHAM
>   Just a moment.

Graham grabs his 8mm Video camera, puts in a new tape, and turns
it on.

>   GRAHAM
>   I am now recording. Tell me your
>   name.

>   CYNTHIA
>   Cynthia Patrice Bishop.

>   GRAHAM
>   Describe for me your first sexual
>   experience.

>   CYNTHIA
>   My first sexual experience or the
>   first time I had intercourse?

>   GRAHAM
>   Your first sexual experience.

>   CYNTHIA
>   (thinks)
>   I was...eight years old. Michael
>   Green, who was also eight, asked
>   if he could watch me take a pee.
>   I said he could if I could watch
>   him take one, too. He said okay,
>   and then we went into the woods
>   behind our house. I got this
>   feeling he was chickening out
>   because he kept saying, "Ladies
>   first!" So I pulled down my
>   underpants and urinated, and he
>   ran away before I even finished.

>   GRAHAM
>   Was it ever a topic of conversation
>   between the two of you afterward?

>   CYNTHIA
>   No. He kind of avoided me for the
>   rest of the summer, and then his
>   family moved away. To Cleveland,
>   actually.

>   (CONTINUED)

24   (CONTINUED) (6)   24

> GRAHAM
> How unfortunate. So when did you
> finally get to see a penis?

> CYNTHIA
> When I was fourteen.

> GRAHAM
> Live, or in a photograph or film
> of some sort?

> CYNTHIA
> Very much live.

> GRAHAM
> What did you think? Did it look
> like you expected?

> CYNTHIA
> Not really. I didn´t picture it
> with veins or ridges or anything,
> I thought it would be smooth, like
> a test tube.

> GRAHAM
> Were you disappointed?

> CYNTHIA
> No. If anything, after I looked
> at it awhile, it got more
> interesting. It had character,
> you know?

> GRAHAM
> What about when you touched it?
> What did you expect it to feel
> like, and then what did it really
> feel like?

> CYNTHIA
> It was warmer than I thought it
> would be, and the skin was softer
> than it looked. It´s weird.
> Thinking about it now, the organ
> itself seemed like a separate
> thing, a separate entity to me.
> I mean, after he pulled it out
> and I could look at it and touch
> it, I <u>completely</u> forgot that there
> was a guy attached to it. I
> remember literally being startled
> when the guy spoke to me.

>   (CONTINUED)

"sex, lies, and videotape"   pg.48

24   (CONTINUED) (7)   24

                         GRAHAM
                What did he say?

                         CYNTHIA
                He said that my hand felt good.

                         GRAHAM
                Then what happened?

                         CYNTHIA
                Then I started moving my hand,
                and then he stopped talking.

25   INT. GRAHAM'S APARTMENT -- DAY   25

        Cynthia, adjusting her clothes, opens the door to leave. She
        looks very aroused. She and Graham do not speak or touch.

26   INT. LAW OFFICES -- DAY   26

        John Millaney picks up a telephone and presses a blinking
        button.

                         JOHN
                John Millaney.

                         CYNTHIA
                I want to see you.

                         JOHN
                When?

                         CYNTHIA
                Right now.

                         JOHN
                Jesus, I don't know if I can get
                away. I've got a client waiting.
                I'd have to do some heavy duty
                juggling.

                         CYNTHIA
                Then get those balls in the air
                and get your butt over here.

        She hangs up. John thinks a moment, then hits his intercom
        button.

                                          (CONTINUED)

26   (CONTINUED)   26

                      JOHN
        Janet, re-schedule Kirkland, see
        if he can come in Friday. Smooth
        things out, tell him an emergency
        came up. I´ll slip out the back.

27   INT. GRAHAM´S APARTMENT -- DAY   27

Graham watches Cynthia´s tape, becoming excited.

                  CYNTHIA
              (voice on tape)
        Would you like me to take my pants
        off?

                  GRAHAM
              (voice on tape)
        If you wish.
              (pause)
        You´re not wearing any underwear.

                  CYNTHIA
              (voice on tape)
        Do you like the way I look?

                  GRAHAM
              (voice on tape)
        Yes.

                  CYNTHIA
              (voice on tape)
        Do you think I´m pretty?

                  GRAHAM
              (voice on tape)
        Yes.

                  CYNTHIA
              (voice on tape)
        Prettier than Ann?

                  GRAHAM
              (voice on tape)
        Different.

28   INT. CYNTHIA BISHOP´S APARTMENT -- DAY   28

Cynthia and John are having sex.

                      (CONTINUED)

"sex, lies, and videotape" pg.50

28   (CONTINUED)   28

                    CYNTHIA
               (to Graham, voice on
                tape)
          John doesn´t have sex with Ann
          anymore.

                    GRAHAM
               (voice on tape)
          Is that what he tells you?

                    CYNTHIA
               (voice on tape)
          He doesn´t have to tell me.

Cynthia has an intense orgasm. She rolls off of John, sweating.

                    JOHN
          Jesus Christ. You are on fire
          today.

Cynthia smiles.

                    CYNTHIA
          Yes. You can go now.

                    DOCTOR
               (voice over)
          If you won´t talk to me, I can´t
          help you.

A moment of silence. John is starting to put his clothes on.
Cynthia lies in bed, her eyes closed, her face serene.

                    ANN
               (voice over)
          I hate my sister.

29   INT. DOCTOR´S OFFICE -- DAY   29

                    DOCTOR
          Why?

                    ANN
               (rambling)
          Because all she thinks about are
          these guys she´s after and I just
          hate her she´s such a little slut
          I thought that in high school and
          I think that now.
                    (more)

> ANN (Cont´d)
> Why do people have to be so
> obsessed with sex all the time,
> what´s the big damn deal? I mean,
> it´s okay and everything, but I
> don´t understand when people let
> it control them, control their
> lives, why do they do that?

30   INT. JOHN AND ANN MILLANEY´S HOUSE -- NIGHT   30

Ann lies awake in bed beside John, who is sound asleep.

> DOCTOR
> (voice over)
> There are many things that can
> exert control over one´s life,
> good and bad. Religion, greed,
> philanthropy, drugs.

> ANN
> (voice over)
> I know, but this...I just feel
> like everybody I know right now
> is obsessed with sex.

Ann looks over at John. She slowly reaches under the covers
and grasps his penis. Without waking, he rolls over and turns
his back to her. She returns to looking at the ceiling.

> ANN
> (voice over)
> Except John, I guess.

31   INT. JOHN AND ANN MILLANEY´S HOUSE -- DAY   31

Ann is talking to Cynthia on the phone. Ann looks very morose.

> CYNTHIA
> He just asked me questions.

> ANN
> What kinds of questions?

> CYNTHIA
> Questions about sex.

> ANN
> Well, like what did he ask,
> exactly?

(CONTINUED)

31   (CONTINUED)   31

                          CYNTHIA
                Well, like, I don´t want to tell
                you, exactly.

                          ANN
                Oh, so you´ll let a total stranger
                record your sexual life on tape,
                but you won´t tell your own sister?

                          CYNTHIA
                Apparently.

                          ANN
                Did he ask you to take your clothes
                off?

                          CYTNHIA
                Did he ask me to take my clothes
                off? No, he didn´t.

A pause.

                          ANN
                Did you take your clothes off?

                          CYNTHIA
                Yes, I did.

                          ANN
                     (floored)
                Cynthia!

                          CYNTHIA
                What!?

                          ANN
                Why did you do that?

                          CYNTHIA
                Because I wanted to.

                          ANN
                But why did you want to?

                          CYNTHIA
                I wanted him to see me.

                          ANN
                Cynthia, who knows where that tape
                may end up? He could be...bouncing
                it off some satellite or something.
                     (more)

                                        (CONTINUED)

31 (CONTINUED) (2) 31

>   ANN (Cont´d)
> Some horny old men in South America
> or something could be watching
> it.
>
>   CYNTHIA
> He wouldn´t do that.
>
>   ANN
> You don´t know that for sure.
>
>   CYNTHIA
> Well, it´s too late now, isn´t
> it?
>
>   ANN
> Did he touch you?
>
>   CYNTHIA
> No, but I did.
>
>   ANN
> You touched <u>him</u>?
>
>   CYTNHIA
> No, I touched <u>me</u>.
>
>   ANN
> Wait a minute. Do you mean...don´t
> tell me you...in front of him.
>
>   CYNTHIA
> In front of him, Ann, yes.
>
>   ANN
>   (serious)
> You are in trouble.
>
>   CYNTHIA
>   (laughs)
> Listen to you!! You sound like
> Mom. What are you talking about?
>
>   ANN
>   (outraged)
> I can´t believe you did that!!
>
>   CYNTHIA
> Why?

                              (CONTINUED)

31   (CONTINUED) (3)   31

                        ANN
          I mean, I couldn't do that in front
          of <u>John</u>, even.

                        CYNTHIA
          You couldn't do it, period.

                        ANN
          You know what I mean, you don't
          even <u>know</u> him!

                        CYNTHIA
          I feel like I do.

                        ANN
          That doesn't mean you <u>do</u>. You can't
          <u>possibly</u> trust him,
          he's...perverted.

                        CYNTHIA
          He's harmless. He just sits around
          and looks at these tapes. What's
          the big deal?

                        ANN
          So he's got this catalogue of women
          touching themselves? That doesn't
          make you feel weird?

                        CYNTHIA
          No. I don't think they <u>all</u> did
          what I did.

                        ANN
          You are in serious trouble.

                        CYNTHIA
          Ann, I don't understand why this
          freaks you out so much. <u>You</u> didn't
          do it, <u>I</u> did, and if it <u>doesn't</u>
          bother me, why should it bother
          you?

                        ANN
          I don't want to discuss it.

                        CYNTHIA
          Then why do you keep asking about
          it?

32   INT. LOUNGE -- DAY   32

A sparse daytime crowd. Cynthia serves a beer to some DUDE.
He puts the money down on the bar and looks at her.

                    DUDE
               (as Marlon Brando)
          Are you an assasin?

                    CYTNHIA
          Excuse me?

                    DUDE
               (still Brando)
          You´re an errand boy...sent by
          grocery clerks...to collect a bill.

Ann enters the lounge, carrying a package.

                    DUDE
               (to Cynthia)
          Brando, it´s Brando, come on.

                    CYNTHIA
          It´s great. Pardon me.

Cynthia moves down the bar to meet Ann.

                    ANN
          I wish you´d get an answering
          machine.

                    CYTNHIA
          There´s a phone here.

                    ANN
          It was busy.

Ann opens the package, revealing a lovely sun dress.

                    ANN
          Here it is.

                    CYNTHIA
          What is it?

                    ANN
          It´s a sun dress.

                    CYNTHIA
          It looks like a tablecloth.

                    ANN
          It does not.

                              (CONTINUED)

"sex, lies, and videotape"   pg.56

32   (CONTINUED)   32

                              CYTNHIA
                    Well, why would she want a sun
                    dress? She´s got spots on her
                    shoulders and varicose veins.

                              ANN
                    So will you, someday.

                              CYNTHIA
                    Yeah, and when I do, I won´t be
                    wearing sun dresses.

The lounge phone rings.

                              ANN
                    I was just trying to--

                              CYNTHIA
                    Hold on.

Cynthia walks to the other end of the bar to answer the phone.
The Dude watches her pass. Then he turns to Ann and gives <u>her</u>
the once-over. He spots the present.

                              DUDE
                    Nice dress.

Ann says nothing.

                              DUDE
                    Wanna hear my Walter Matthau?
                    You´ll love this.
                         (as Matthau)
                    "Feeelix, what are you, craaazee?"
                         (back to normal)
                    Pretty good, huh?

Cynthia picks up the phone.

                              CYNTHIA
                    Hello.

                              JOHN
                    Cynthia. John.

                              CYNTHIA
                    Well, this is timely. Your wife
                    is here, would you like to speak
                    to her?

                                        (CONTINUED)

32   (CONTINUED) (2)   32

                          JOHN
              She´s there? What´s she doing
              there?

                          CYTNHIA
              She came by to show me a present
              that she and I are buying for your
              mother-in-law.

                          JOHN
              Oh. When can I see you?

                          CYNTHIA
              I don´t know. I´m not sure I can
              duplicate the level of intensity
              I had the other day.

                          JOHN
              Nothing wrong with trying.

                          CYNTHIA
              I don´t think my sister would
              agree.

A pause.

                          JOHN
              Do you want me to stop calling?

                          CYNTHIA
              Look, I´ll call you, okay?

Cynthia hangs up and walks back to Ann.

                          CYTNHIA
              So what´s my share of the dress?

                          ANN
              Thirty-two dollars.

Cynthia pulls thirty-five bucks out of her jeans. She watches
Ann put the money away.

                          CYNTHIA
              Look, don´t worry about the dress,
              I´m sure she´ll love it.

                          DUDE
                   (to Ann and Cynthia)
              Hey!! How about Tom Brokaw? Nobody
              does Brokaw.
                   (as Tom Brokaw)
              "In Iran today..."

"sex, lies, and videotape"   pg.58

33   SCENE DELETED   33

34   INT. GRAHAM´S APARTMENT -- DAY   34

Graham sits reading a book. There is a knock at his door.

                    GRAHAM
          It´s open.

Cynthia enters the room, looking very intent on something.

                    GRAHAM
          Hello.

                    CYNTHIA
          Hi.

Graham sets his book down. He looks at her for a moment, then
drags on his cigarette.

                    CYNTHIA
          Look, I´m just going to come right
          out and tell you why I´m here,
          okay?

                    GRAHAM
          Okay.

                    CYNTHIA
          I´d like to make another tape.

Graham thinks for a moment.

                    GRAHAM
          No.

                    CYNTHIA
          No? Not even one more?

                    GRAHAM
          I never do more than one. I´m
          sorry.

                    CYNTHIA
          I can´t talk you into it?

                    GRAHAM
          No. You´ll have to get somebody
          else.

                    CYNTHIA
          Now who the hell is going to do
          that for me?

                              (CONTINUED)

34   (CONTINUED)   34

                         GRAHAM
          I´m sure a substantial number of
          men in this town would volunteer.

                         CYNTHIA
          But I want you to do it, I want
          somebody who will ask the right
          questions and everything, somebody
          I can play to and feel safe because
          you can´t do anything.

                         GRAHAM
          Ouch. Okay, I deserved that.
          Cynthia, don´t you understand?
          After the first time it´s just
          not spontaneous. There´s no edge
          anymore. Look at the tapes, there
          is only one date on each label.
          I have never taped anyone twice.

                         CYNTHIA
          So make an exception.

                         GRAHAM
          No.

                         CYNTHIA
          How about if you record over the
          one we already made? You could
          have the same date and not use
          another tape. Who would know?

                         GRAHAM
          I would.

                         CYNTHIA
          Well, what the hell am I supposed
          to do?

                         GRAHAM
          Cynthia, I don´t know.

                         CYNTHIA
          I can´t believe you´re doing this
          after I let you tape me.

                         GRAHAM
          I´m sorry. I can´t do it.

                         CYNTHIA
          Goddamit, give me my tape, then.

                                        (CONTINUED)

"sex, lies, and videotape"   pg.60

34   (CONTINUED) (2)   34

                         GRAHAM
             No.

Cynthia heads for the tape box. Graham leaps up to stop her.

                         CYNTHIA
                    (digging through the
                    box)
             It´s <u>my</u> fucking tape, you asshole--

Graham grabs her wrists momentarily.

                         GRAHAM
                    (heated)
             No!! I told you what the parameters
             were and you agreed. It´s <u>my</u> tape.
             <u>I</u> look at it, <u>I</u> touch it, nobody
             else.

Cynthia and Graham look at each other for a long moment.

                         GRAHAM
             Please go, I´d like you to go now.

Cynthia looks at him.

                         CYNTHIA
             Sure, okay.

She leaves.

35   INT. JOHN AND ANN MILLANEY´S HOUSE -- NIGHT   35

John and Ann lie in bed. The lights are out. Ann is wide awake,
while John is on the verge of sleep. He rolls over and puts his
arm around her. She gets up and sits in a chair opposite the
bed.

                         ANN
             John?

                         JOHN
             Mmmmm...

                         ANN
             I called you Tuesday at 3:30 and
             they said you weren´t in. Do you
             remember where you were?

                                        (CONTINUED)

"sex, lies, and videotape"   pg.61

35   (CONTINUED)   35

      CUT TO:

36   INT. CYNTHIA BISHOP´S APARTMENT -- DAY   36

      John and Cynthia are in Cynthia´s bed, kissing. On the floor,
      John´s watch reads 3:11 pm.

      CUT BACK TO:

37   INT. JOHN AND ANN MILLANEY´S HOUSE -- NIGHT   37

                          JOHN
                  Tuesday. I had a late lunch.

                          ANN
                  Did you see a message to call me
                  when you got back in?

      CUT TO:

38   EXT. CYNTHIA BISHOP´S HOUSE -- DAY   38

      John leaves Cynthia´s house and drives straight home, greeting
      Ann as he steps through the front door.

      CUT BACK TO:

39   INT. JOHN AND ANN MILLANEY´S HOUSE -- NIGHT   39

                          JOHN
                  Yes. I just got busy.

                          ANN
                  That´s interesting, because I
                  didn´t leave a message.

      John is waking up a little.

                          JOHN
                  Then maybe I saw an old message.
                  There are a lot of them on my desk,
                  you know.

                          ANN
                  Who´d you have lunch with?

                          JOHN
                  I ate by myself.

                                          (CONTINUED)

39   (CONTINUED)   39

A pause.

                         JOHN
          Something wrong?

                         ANN
          Are you having an affair?

                         JOHN
          Jesus Christ, where´d that come
          from? I have a late lunch by
          myself and now I´m fucking
          somebody?

                         ANN
          Well, are you?

                         JOHN
          <u>No</u>, I´m not. Frankly, I´m offended
          at the accusation.

                         ANN
          If I´m right, I want to know.
          I don´t want you to lie. I´d be
          very upset, but not as upset as
          if I´d found out you´d been lying.

                         JOHN
          There´s nothing to know, Ann.

                         ANN
          I can´t tell you how upset I would
          be if you were lying.

                         JOHN
          Ann, you are <u>completely</u> paranoid.
          Not ten minutes ago <u>I</u> wanted to
          make love for the first time in
          weeks, and <u>you</u> act like I´m dipped
          in shit. You know, I think there
          are a lot of women that would be
          glad to have a young, straight
          male making a pretty good living
          beside them in bed with a hard
          on.

                         ANN
          My sister, for one. Is that who
          it is?

                              (CONTINUED)

39   (CONTINUED) (2)   39

               JOHN
For God´s sake, Ann, I am <u>not</u>
fucking your sister. I don´t find
her that attractive, for one.

               ANN
Is that supposed to comfort me?

               JOHN
I was just <u>saying</u>, you know? I
didn´t get paranoid when you didn´t
want to make love. I could have
easily assumed that you didn´t
want to because <u>you</u> were having
an affair.

               ANN
But I´m not.

               JOHN
I´m not either!!

               ANN
Why don´t I believe you?

               JOHN
Look, this conversation is utterly
ridiculous. Maybe when you have
some evidence, we should talk,
but don´t give me conjecture and
intuition.

               ANN
Always the lawyer.

               JOHN
Goddam right. I mean, can you
imagine: "Your honor, I´m <u>positive</u>
this man is guilty. I can´t place
him at the scene or establish a
<u>motive</u>, but I have this really
strong <u>feeling</u>."

               ANN
You´ve made your point.

                         (CONTINUED)

39   (CONTINUED) (3)   39

                         JOHN
          I´m sorry. It´s just...I´m under
          a lot of pressure with this
          Kirkland thing, it´s my first big
          case as junior partner, and I work
          all day, I come home, I look
          forward to seeing you, and...it
          hurts that you accuse me like that.

A pause. Ann exhales.

                         ANN
          I´m sorry, too. I...I get these
          ideas in my head, you know, and
          I have nothing to do all day but
          sit around and concoct these
          intricate scenarios. And then
          I want to believe it so I don´t
          think I´ve wasted the whole day.
          Last week I was convinced you were
          having an affair with Cynthia,
          I don´t know why.

                         JOHN
          I don´t, either. I mean, <u>Cynthia</u>,
          of all people. She´s so...

                         ANN
          Loud.

                         JOHN
          Yeah. Jeez, give me some credit.

                         ANN
          I didn´t say it was rational, I
          just said I was convinced.

                         JOHN
          Isn´t therapy helping at all?

                         ANN
          I don´t know. Sometimes I feel
          stupid babbling about my little
          problems while children are
          starving in the world.

                         JOHN
          Quitting your therapy won´t feed
          the children of Ethiopia.

                         ANN
          I know.

                                        (CONTINUED)

39   (CONTINUED) (4)   39

A pause.

                    ANN
          You never used to say "fucking".

40   SCENE DELETED   40

41   INT. CYNTHIA BISHOP´S -- DAY   41

John sits on the edge of Cynthia´s bed, slowly undressing.

                    JOHN
          It´s just so blatantly stupid,
          I have a hard time believing you
          did it.

                    CYNTHIA
          What´s so stupid about it?

                    JOHN
          That you...you don´t even know
          the guy.

                    CYNTHIA
          Well, you know him, he´s a friend
          of yours, do you think he can be
          trusted?

                    JOHN
          Shit, after what you´ve told me,
          I don´t know. I should´ve known,
          when he showed up dressed like
          some arty brat.

                    CYNTHIA
          I like the way he dresses.

                    JOHN
          What if this tape gets into the
          wrong hands?

                    CYNTHIA
          "The wrong hands"? We´re not
          talking about military secrets,
          John. They´re just tapes that he
          makes so he can sit around and
          get   off.

                              (CONTINUED)

41   (CONTINUED)   41

                    JOHN
           Jesus Christ. And he doesn't have
           sex with <u>any</u> of them? They just
           talk?

                  CYNTHIA
           Right.

                    JOHN
           Jesus. I could almost understand
           it if he was screwing these people,
           <u>almost</u>. Why doesn't he just buy
           some magazines or porno movies
           or something?

                  CYNTHIA
           Doesn't work. He has to know the
           people, he has to be able to
           interact with them.

                    JOHN
           Interact, fine, but did you have
           to masturbate in front of him,
           for God's sake? I mean......

                  CYNTHIA
           I felt like it, so what? Goddam,
           you and Ann make such a big deal
           out of it.
A pause.

                    JOHN
           You told <u>Ann</u> about this?

                  CYNTHIA
           Of course. She <u>is</u> my sister. I
           tell her <u>almost</u> everything.

                    JOHN
           I wish you hadn't done that.

                  CYNTHIA
           Why not?

                    JOHN
           It's just something I'd prefer
           she didn't know about.

                  CYNTHIA
           She's a grown-up, she can handle
           it.

                    (CONTINUED)

41   (CONTINUED) (2)   41

                         JOHN
             I just...Ann is very...

                       CYNTHIA
             Hung up.

                         JOHN
             It just wasn´t a smart thing to
             do. Did you sign any sort of
             paper, or did he have any contract
             with you saying he wouldn´t
             broadcast these tapes?

                       CYNTHIA
             No.

                         JOHN
             You realize you have no recourse
             legally? This stuff could show
             up anywhere.

                       CYNTHIA
             It won´t. I trust him.

                         JOHN
                    (disbelieving)
             You trust him.

                       CYNTHIA
             Yeah, I do. A helluva lot more
             than I trust you.

                         JOHN
             What do you mean?

                       CYNTHIA
             Exactly what I said. I´d trust
             him before I´d trust you. How much
             clearer can I be?

                         JOHN
             It hurts that you would say that
             to me.

                       CYNTHIA
                    (laughs)
             Oh, please. Come on, John. You´re
             fucking your wife´s sister and
             you hardly been married a year.
             You´re a liar. But at least I know
             you´re a liar.
                       (more)

                                      (CONTINUED)

41   (CONTINUED) (3)   41

                        CYNTHIA (Cont´d)
            It´s the people that <u>don´t</u> know,
            like Ann, that have to watch out.

                        JOHN
            By definition you´re lying to Ann,
            too.

                        CYNTHIA
            That´s right. But I never took
            a vow in front of God and everybody
            to be "faithful" to my sister.

                        JOHN
            Look, are we going to do it or
            not?

                        CYNTHIA
            Actually, no, I´ve changed my mind.
            I shouldn´t have called.

                        JOHN
                (ingratiating)
            Well, I´m here now. I´d like to
            do something...

                        CYNTHIA
            How about straightening up the
            living room?

John doesn´t smile.

                        CYNTHIA
            Come on, John. You should be happy,
            we´ve gone this far without Ann
            finding out, I´m making it real
            easy on you. Just walk out of here
            and I´ll see you at your house
            for a family dinner sometime.

                        JOHN
            Did he put you up to this?

                        CYNTHIA
            Who?

                        JOHN
            Graham.

                                    (CONTINUED)

41   (CONTINUED) (4)   41

                         CYNTHIA
          No, he didn´t put me up to this.
          Jesus, I don´t need people to tell
          me what I should do. I´ve just
          been thinking about things, that´s
          all.

                         JOHN
          I can´t believe I let him stay
          in my house. Right under my nose.
          That deviant fucker was right under
          my nose and I didn´t see him.

                         CYNTHIA
          If he had been under your prick
          you´d have spotted him for sure.

                         JOHN
                 (looks at her)
          God, you....you´re mean.

                         CYNTHIA
          I know. Will you please leave now?

                         JOHN
          Maybe I don´t want to leave. Maybe
          I want to talk.

                         CYNTHIA
          John, we have nothing to talk
          about.

                         JOHN
          I knew it, I knew it. Things are
          getting complicated.

                         CYNTHIA
          No, John, things are getting real
          simple.

42   INT. JOHN AND ANN MILLANEY´S HOUSE -- DAY   42

Ann, dressed in some of John´s work clothes (old cotton shirt,
khaki pants) is cleaning the house. Not cleaning like a normal
person, but like an obsessive/compulsive person. Scrubbing spots
that are already clean, vacuuming the same area of rug over
and over, etc. Suddenly, an object lodges itself in the snout
of the vacuum cleaner, making a loud noise. Shutting the machine
off, Ann turns it over and sees that Cynthia´s diamond stud
earring has gotten hooked in the take-up roller.

                                        (CONTINUED)

"sex, lies, and videotape"   pg.70

42   (CONTINUED)   42

Ann stares at Cynthia´s earring for a long moment.

CUT TO:

Cynthia picking up her jacket from beside the bed after having
sex with John. The earring slips out of the pocket and bounces
under the edge of the bed.

CUT BACK TO:

Ann as she sets the earring onto the floor and begins to pound
it with the bottom of a water glass, trying to smash it to
pieces. She soon realizes the futility of trying to break a
diamond.

Ann looks down at herself. Suddenly realizing that she is
dressed in John´s clothing, she frantically rips the shirt and
pants from her body as though the material were burning her
skin. Popped buttons skid across the floor.

Clothed only in her bra and underwear, Ann sits in the middle
of the bedroom floor, arms around herself.

43   EXT. JOHN AND ANN MILLANEY´S HOUSE -- DAY   43

Ann, now in jeans and t-shirt, stumbles to her car. Once inside,
she jams the key into the ignition and rests her head against
the steering wheel.

44   EXT. GRAHAM´S APARTMENT -- DAY   44

Ann lifts her head from the steering wheel and looks up. She
looks almost surprised to find that she has driven to Graham´s.
Slowly, she gets out of the car.

45   INT. GRAHAM´S APARTMENT -- DAY   45

Graham sits reading.

There is a weak knock at the door. Graham listens, not sure he
heard anything. There is a second weak knock.

                         GRAHAM
               It´s open!

Nothing happens. Graham gets up and opens the door himself.
Ann stands against the wall of the hallway, her head down, her
breathing deliberate. Concerned, Graham slowly begins to lead
her inside. Impulsively, she hugs him tightly.

                              (CONTINUED)

45   (CONTINUED)   45

Unaccustomed to physical contact, Graham's hands hang awkwardly
at his side. Ann slowly pulls back from the embrace and sits
down. Graham goes to the kitchen area and gets her a glass of
water. He gives it to her and sits in the chair opposite. Ann
holds the glass in her hand, staring at it.

                    GRAHAM
          It's bottled, not tap.

A weak smile from Ann. She drinks, swallowing with difficulty.

                    ANN
          I'm not sure why I came here. I
          had kind of decided not to talk
          to you after...you know.

                    GRAHAM
          I know.

A pause.

                    ANN
          That son of a <u>bitch</u>.

Ann looks at Graham.

                    ANN
              (sarcastic)
          John and Cynthia have been...
          "fucking".

                    GRAHAM
          I know.

                    ANN
              (stunned)
          You <u>know</u>?

                    GRAHAM
          Yes.

                    ANN
          How did you know?

                    GRAHAM
          She said it on her tape.

                    ANN
              (angry)
          Why didn't you tell me?

                                        (CONTINUED)

45   (CONTINUED) (2)   45

                         GRAHAM
             Ann, when would I have told you?
             We were not speaking, if you
             recall.

Ann says nothing.

                         GRAHAM
             But even if we had been speaking,
             I wouldn't have told you.

                         ANN
             Why not?

                         GRAHAM
             It's not my place to tell you these
             things, Ann. You have to find out
             by yourself or from John directly.
             You have to trust me on this.

Ann shakes her head.

                         ANN
             My life is...shit. It's all shit.
             It's like somebody saying, "Okay,
             chairs are not chairs, they're
             actually swimming pools". I mean,
             nothing is what I thought it was.
             What happened to me? Have I been
             asleep? I vaguely remember the
             wedding, but a lot of it is just
             a blur... like I was watching
             from a distance. I can't <u>believe</u>
             him. Why didn't I trust my
             intuition?

Graham says nothing.

                         ANN
             And I'm vacuuming his goddam rug.
             <u>His</u> rug, that<u>he</u> paid to have put
             in <u>his</u> house. Nothing in that place
             belongs to me. I wanted to put
             some of my grandmother's furniture
             in it, but he wouldn't let me.
             So I'm vacuuming <u>his</u> rug. That
             bastard.

Ann looks at Graham.

                         ANN
             I want to make a tape.

                                    (CONTINUED)

45   (CONTINUED) (3)   45

A pause.

                    GRAHAM
          Do you think that´s such a good
          idea?

                    ANN
          Don´t you want to make one?

                    GRAHAM
          Yes. But I sense the element of
          revenge here.

                    ANN
          What difference does it make <u>why</u>
          I do it?

                    GRAHAM
          I want you to be aware of what
          you´re doing and why, because I
          know that this is not the sort
          of thing you would do in a normal
          frame of mind.

                    ANN
          What would you know about a normal
          frame of mind?

                    GRAHAM
               (impressed)
          That´s a good question.

                    ANN
          What do you have to do to get
          ready?

                    GRAHAM
          Load a new tape, turn the camera
          on.

                    ANN
          Then do it.

Graham opens a new box of videotapes.

                    ANN
          How do you pay for all this? I
          mean, rent, and tapes and this
          equipment.

                    GRAHAM
          I have money.

                              (CONTINUED)

"sex, lies, and videotape"   pg.74

45   (CONTINUED)   (4)   45

                         ANN
              What will you do when the money
              runs out?

                         GRAHAM
              It won´t. Are you ready?

                         ANN
              Yes.

Graham turns the camera on.

                         GRAHAM
              Tell me your name.

                         ANN
              Ann Bishop Millaney.

CUT TO BLACK:

THEN CUT TO:

46   EXT. GRAHAM´S APARTMENT -- DUSK   46

Street lights are illuminated. Night is imminent.

47   INT. GRAHAM´S APARTMENT -- DUSK   47

Graham stops the video recorder. The record meter is stopped at
46:02.

Ann sits beside Graham on the couch. She looks into his eyes,
stroking his hair.

After a moment, she gets up to leave.

48   INT. JOHN AND ANN MILLANEY´S HOUSE -- NIGHT   48

John is talking on the phone as Ann walks through the door.
He mumbles an apology into the receiver and hangs up as Ann
moves to the couch, her expression calm.

                         JOHN
                       (worried)
              Jesus Christ! What the hell
              happened?
                        (more)

                                             (CONTINUED)

48   (CONTINUED)   48

>   JOHN (Cont´d)
>   I came home and your car was gone,
>   the door was open, I thought for
>   sure you´d been abducted by some
>   mad fucker, I was literally just
>   calling the cops when you walked
>   in. What happened?
>
>   ANN
>   I want out of this marriage.
>
>   JOHN
>   (genuinely shocked)
>   What?
>
>   ANN
>   (looks at him)
>   I want out of this marriage.
>
>   JOHN
>   Why?
>
>   ANN
>   We´ll call it uncontested or
>   whatever. I just want out.

John moves to sit beside her on the couch. Ann does not look
at him.

>   JOHN
>   (conciliatory)
>   Ann, honey, please, tell me what´s
>   wrong. Don´t just say you want
>   out and leave me wondering. You
>   can´t just <u>go</u> without telling me
>   why.

Ann turns to look at him for a moment, then turns away.

>   ANN
>   Fuck you. I can do what I want.

John´s mouth literally hangs open in shock. He is dumbstruck.

>   ANN
>   I´ll stay at my mother´s.

John gets up from the couch and begins pacing.

>   JOHN
>   Where did you go when you left
>   here?

>   (CONTINUED)

48   (CONTINUED) (2)   48

> ANN
> I drove around. Then I went to
> talk with Graham.

John smacks his hand on his leg.

> JOHN
> Goddammit, goddammit!! That son
> of a bitch!!
>   (thinking)
> Well, at least I know you didn't
> fuck him.

> ANN
> No, but I <u>wanted</u> to. I <u>really</u>
> wanted to, <u>partially</u> just to piss
> you off.

John is seething.

> JOHN
> You're leaving me for him, aren't
> you? Well, that makes a sad sort
> of sense. He can't, and you won't.

> ANN
> I'm not going to discuss this with
> you anymore. You're making no
> sense.

John walks over to Ann.

> JOHN
> Did you make one of those goddam
> tapes?

Ann says nothing.

> JOHN
> <u>Answer</u> me, godammit!! Did you make
> <u>one of</u> those tapes?

> ANN
> Yes!

John explodes, hitting the wall all around Ann. She cowers
beneath the storm.

John bolts from the house.

> ANN
> DON'T YOU TOUCH HIM!!!

49   INT. GRAHAM´S APARTMENT -- NIGHT   49

Graham stands in the middle of the room with a cigarette in
his mouth, trying to teach himself to moonwalk.

50   EXT. GRAHAM´S APARTMENT -- NIGHT   50

John screeches to a halt, parking haphazardly. He gets out of
the car and runs to Graham´s apartment.

51   INT. GRAHAM´S APARTMENT -- NIGHT   51

John bursts through the door without bothering to knock. Graham
looks up, startled. Before he can even react, John has him by
the lapels.

                    GRAHAM
               Hi, John.

                    JOHN
               Where are the tapes, Graham?

                    GRAHAM
               What tapes?

                    JOHN
               You know which tapes! Where are
               they?

                    GRAHAM
               John, as a lawyer, you should know
               that those tapes are private
               property.

                    JOHN
               So is my wife, asshole!!

                    GRAHAM
               She´s not property, John, she´s
               person. Were you just going to
               keep right on lying to her?

                    JOHN
               What the hell do you think? I
               love Ann. You think I´m going to
               tell her about Cynthia and hurt
               her feelings like that?

                    GRAHAM
               God, you need help.

                                        (CONTINUED)

"sex, lies, and videotape"   pg.78

51   (CONTINUED)   51

                         JOHN
               I need help? Whose sitting by
               himself in a room choking his
               chauncey to a bunch of videotapes,
               Graham? Not me, buddy. You're the
               fucking nut. Now show me those
               tapes.

                         GRAHAM
               No.

                         JOHN
               I'm not kidding, Graham, you'd
               better do what I say. Give me those
               tapes.

                         GRAHAM
               No.

John punches Graham in the jaw, knocking him to the floor.
Graham feels his mouth for blood as John picks him up by the
shirt.

                         JOHN
               Graham, I swear to Christ I'll
               kill your scrawny ass. Now give
               me those tapes.

                         GRAHAM
               No.

John roughly pushes Graham into one of the director's chairs,
which topples over and throws Graham to the floor once again.

John looks around. He sees the boxes of tapes and begins to
go through the contents. Graham gets up and runs over to stop
him.

                         GRAHAM
               Get away from those!! They belong
               to me!!

Graham and John struggle. John hits Graham in the stomach and
pushes him to the floor.

                         JOHN
               Give me your keys.

                         GRAHAM
               My keys?

John bends over and starts going through Graham's pockets.

                              (CONTINUED)

51   (CONTINUED) (2)   51

                          JOHN
          Your keys, asshole!! Your <u>two</u>
          fucking keys!! Give them to me!!

                        GRAHAM
          I´m not going to give you my keys.

John beats Graham until Graham can offer no resistance. He then
drags Graham into the hallway and leaves him there.

John then locks himself inside Graham´s apartment.

John walks over to the boxes of videotapes and begins to search
through them spastically. He finds both Cynthia and Ann´s tapes.
After a brief deliberation, he decides to watch Ann´s. He turns
on the player and the monitor. After pulling a chair up to the
screen, John presses the button marked "play".

In the hallway, Graham drags himself to the door of his
apartment. Putting his ear to the inlet, he strains to hear
what is going on inside.

John watches the monitor come to life.

The image is Ann, sitting in a chair.

                        GRAHAM
                 (on tape)
          Tell me your name.

                        ANN
                 (on tape)
          Ann Bishop Millaney.

                        GRAHAM
                 (on tape)
          You are married, correct?

                        JOHN
          Goddam right.

                        ANN
                 (on tape)
         Yes.

                        GRAHAM
                 (on tape)
         Who usually initiates sex?

John´s jaw tightens.

                                (CONTINUED)

51   (CONTINUED) (3)   51

>   JOHN
>   Bastard...
>
>   ANN
>   (on tape)
>   He does.
>
>   GRAHAM
>   (on tape)
>   Do you talk to him?
>
>   ANN
>   (on tape)
>   When we´re making love?
>
>   GRAHAM
>   (on tape)
>   Yes.
>
>   ANN
>   (on tape)
>   Sometimes. Afterward.
>
>   GRAHAM
>   (on tape)
>   Does he go down on you?
>
>   JOHN
>   (shouting at Graham)
>   You son of a bitch!!
>
>   ANN
>   (on tape)
>   Not very often.
>
>   GRAHAM
>   (on tape)
>   I would.

John is literally so mad he can´t speak. He watches the screen
in mute anger, his hands wrapped tightly around the arms of
the chair. Graham still listens from the hallway.

>   GRAHAM
>   (on tape)
>   Have you ever wanted to make love
>   to someone other than your husband?
>
>   JOHN
>   Goddamit...

Ann hesitates.

>   (CONTINUED)

51   (CONTINUED) (4)   51

                    JOHN
                (to Ann´s image)
            Answer him, goddammit!!

                    GRAHAM
                (on tape)
            You´re hesitating. I think that
            means you have.

                    JOHN
                (to Graham on tape)
            Shut up!!!

                    ANN
                (on tape)
            You don´t know what I´m thinking.

                    GRAHAM
                (on tape)
            It´s a simple question. Have you
            ever <u>thought</u> of having--making
            love <u>with</u> someone other than your
            husband?

John leans forward.

                    ANN
                (on tape)
            Is he going to see this?

                    GRAHAM
                (on tape)
            Absolutely not.

A sarcastic chuckle from John. In the hallway, Graham furrows
his brow.

                    ANN
                (on tape)
            I have <u>thought</u> about it, yes.

                    JOHN
                (to Ann´s image)
            You bitch. I <u>knew</u> it.

                    GRAHAM
                (on tape)
            Did you have sex before you were
            married?

                                    (CONTINUED)

"sex, lies, and videotape"   pg.82

51   (CONTINUED) (5)   51

                        ANN
                     (on tape)
          Yes.

                        GRAHAM
                     (on tape)
          Did the person you made love with
          satisfy you more than your husband?

                        JOHN
                     (to Graham)
          God damn you!!

                        ANN
                     (on tape)
          Yes.

John stands and throws his chair against the door. Graham, still
listening at the door, is startled.

                        GRAHAM
                     (on tape)
          And you have thought about...making
          love to that person again since
          you've been married?

John watches the monitor, his eyes beginning to water.

                        ANN
                     (on tape)
          I don't see what difference it
          makes, I mean, I can <u>think</u> what
          I want.
                     (pause)
          I don't know if I want to do this
          anymore, I'm afraid...I don't mind
          answering the questions so much,
          but if somebody were to <u>see</u> this...

                        GRAHAM
                     (on tape)
          At some level, I don't understand
          your nervousness. Have you decided
          to leave John?

Ann thinks. John watches.

                        ANN
                     (on tape)
          Yes, I have. I will.

                              (CONTINUED)

51   (CONTINUED) (6)   51

                    GRAHAM
                   (on tape)
          Then as far as this taping goes,
          you have nothing to worry about.

                    ANN
                   (on tape)
          I guess not.

                    GRAHAM
                   (on tape)
          Do you want me to stop?

John, absorbed in the image, absently shakes his head.

                    ANN
                   (on tape)
          No.

                    GRAHAM
                   (on tape)
          Are there people other than your
          previous lover that you have
          fantasized about?

A pause.

                    ANN
                   (on tape)
          Yes. Whenever...all right, look.
          Whenever I see a man that I think
          is attractive, I wonder what it
          would be like with him, I mean,
          I´m just curious, I don´t act on
          it, but I <u>hate</u> that I think that!!
          I wish I <u>could</u> just forget about
          that stuff!!

                    GRAHAM
                   (on tape)
          Why?

                    ANN
                   (on tape)
          Because that´s how Cynthia thinks!!
          All she does is think about that
          stuff, and I hate that, I don´t
          want to be like her, I <u>don´t</u> want
          to be like her!!

                                        (CONTINUED)

51   (CONTINUED) (7)   51

>   GRAHAM
>   (on tape)
>   You´re not like your sister. You
>   couldn´t be like her if you <u>wanted</u>
>   to.

>   ANN
>   (on tape)
>   I know. Deep down, I know that.
>   It just bothers me, when I have
>   feelings or impulses that <u>she</u> has.

John picks up the chair he threw and sets it upright. He sits
down and watches the screen impassively. Graham still listens
from outside.

>   GRAHAM
>   (on tape)
>   So you do fantasize?

>   ANN
>   (on tape)
>   Yes.

>   GRAHAM
>   (on tape)
>   About who?

>   ANN
>   (on tape)
>   I fantasized about you.

>   GRAHAM
>   (on tape)
>   About me?

>   ANN
>   (on tape)
>   Yes.

A pause.

>   ANN
>   (on tape)
>   Have you fantasized about me?

>   GRAHAM
>   (on tape)
>   I thought I made that clear before,
>   when I said I would go down on
>   you.

>   (CONTINUED)

51   (CONTINUED) (8)   51

                         ANN
                      (on tape)
              I remember. You <u>could</u> do that,
              couldn´t you? Go <u>down</u> on me?

                         GRAHAM
                      (on tape)
              Yes.

                         ANN
                      (on tape)
              If I asked you to, would you? Not
              on tape, I mean?

                         GRAHAM
                      (on tape)
              No.

                         ANN
                      (on tape)
              On tape?

                         GRAHAM
                      (on tape)
              No.

                         ANN
                      (on tape)
              Why not?

                         GRAHAM
                      (on tape)
              If I can´t do it all, I don´t want
              to do anything. And I can´t do
              it all.

                         ANN
                      (on tape)
              Can´t or won´t?

A pause. John is still watching the tape, his face betraying
no emotion. Graham still listens from outside.

CUT TO:

The previous afternoon. We are no longer looking at Ann on the
monitor, but watching her and Graham AS THEY MADE THE TAPE. For
instance, we can now see Graham from Ann´s point of view, or the
two of them at the same time, etc.

                         GRAHAM
              Can´t.

                                        (CONTINUED)

51   (CONTINUED) (9)   51

                    ANN
          You said you weren´t always
          impotent.

                    GRAHAM
          That´s correct.

                    ANN
          So you <u>have</u> had sex.

                    GRAHAM
          Yes.

                    ANN
          Who was the last person you had
          sex with?

                    GRAHAM
          Her name was Elizabeth.

                    ANN
          So what happened? Was it so bad
          that it turned you off?

                    GRAHAM
          No, it was wonderful. That wasn´t
          the problem.

                    ANN
          What was the problem?

                    GRAHAM
          The problem was me. I was...I was
          a pathological liar. Or <u>am</u>, I
          should say. Lying is like
          alcoholism, one is always
          "recovering".

                    ANN
          So you lied to her?

                    GRAHAM
          Yes. I did. Willfully and
          repeatedly.

                    ANN
          How come?

                              (CONTINUED)

51   (CONTINUED) (10)   51

                        GRAHAM
          I loved her for how good she made
          me feel, and I hated her for how
          good she made me feel. And at that
          time, I tended to express my
          feelings non-verbally. I couldn't
          handle anyone having that much
          control over my emotions.

                        ANN
          And now you can?

                        GRAHAM
          Now I make sure that no one has
          the opportunity to test me.

                        ANN
          Don't you get lonely?

                        GRAHAM
          How could I, with all these nice
          people stopping by? The fact is
          that I've lived by myself for so
          long, I can't imagine living with
          another person. It's amazing what
          you can get used to if enough time
          goes by. And anyway, I'm asking
          the questions. Are you happy?

                        ANN
          I don't know anymore. I thought
          I was, but obviously I was wrong.

                        GRAHAM
          Did you confront John with the
          fact that you knew about him?

                        ANN
          Not yet. I'm not sure I will. I
          just want out.

                        GRAHAM
          If you do get out of your marriage,
          will you continue to be inhibited?

                        ANN
          I don't know. It all gets back
          to that Cynthia thing. I don't
          like her...eagerness. There's
          nothing left to imagine, there's
          no...

                                        (CONTINUED)

51   (CONTINUED) (11)   51

                         GRAHAM
          Subtlety?

                         ANN
          Subtlety, yes. No subtlety. Plus,
          I've never really felt able to
          open up with anyone. I mean, that
          other person I told you about,
          I enjoyed making love with him
          a lot, but I still wasn't able
          to really let go. I always feel
          like I'm being watched and I
          shouldn't embarrass myself.

                         GRAHAM
          And you feel the same way with
          John?

                         ANN
          Kind of. I mean, John's like this
          kind of...craftsman. Like he's
          a carpenter, and he makes really
          good tables. But that's all he
          can make, and I don't need anymore
          tables.

                         GRAHAM
          Interesting analogy.

                         ANN
          I'm babbling.

                         GRAHAM
          No, you're not.

                         ANN
               (thinking)
          God, I'm so mad at him!!

                         GRAHAM
          You should be. He lied to you.
          So did Cynthia.

                         ANN
          Yeah, I know, but somehow I expect
          that from her, I mean, she'll do
          it with almost anybody, I don't
          know, I shouldn't stick up for
          her I guess, but him. He lied
          so...deeply!! Ooo, I want to watch
          him die!!

                                   (CONTINUED)

"sex, lies, and videotape"

51   (CONTINUED) (12)   51

Ann sits quietly for a moment. Graham watches her silently. The camera continues to roll.

>   ANN
>   (looks up at Graham)
>   You´re really never going to make
>   love again?

>   GRAHAM
>   I´m not planning on it.

A pause.

>   ANN
>   If you were in love with me, would
>   you?

>   GRAHAM
>   I´m not in love with you.

>   ANN
>   But if you were?

>   GRAHAM
>   I...I can´t answer that precisely.

>   ANN
>   But I feel like maybe I could be
>   really comfortable with you.

>   GRAHAM
>   That´s very flattering.

>   ANN
>   So why won´t you make love with
>   me? Why <u>wouldn´t</u> you, I mean?

>   GRAHAM
>   Ann. Are you asking me
>   hypothetically, or are you asking
>   me for real, right now?

>   ANN
>   I´m asking for real. I want you
>   to turn that camera off and make
>   love with me. Will you?

A pause.

>   GRAHAM
>   I can´t.

(CONTINUED)

51   (CONTINUED) (13)   51

                              ANN
                    Why not?

                              GRAHAM
                    I´ve told you.

                              ANN
                    But I don´t understand--

                              GRAHAM
                    Ann, it could happen to me all
                    over again, don´t you see? I could
                    start to--

                              ANN
                    But how do you know for sure, you
                    have to try to find a way to fig--

                              GRAHAM
                    I couldn´t face her if I had slept
                    with somebody else.

        A pause.

                              ANN
                    Who? Elizabeth?

                              GRAHAM
                         (uncomfortable)
                    Yes.

                              ANN
                    You mean you´re still in contact
                    with her?

                              GRAHAM
                    No.

                              ANN
                    But you´re planning to be?

                              GRAHAM
                    I don´t know. Possibly.

                              ANN
                    Wait a minute, wait a minute.
                    What´s going on here? Did you come
                    back here just to see her again?

                              GRAHAM
                    Not entirely.

                                        (CONTINUED)

51   (CONTINUED) (14)   51

              ANN
But that was part of it?

              GRAHAM
Yes.

              ANN
Like maybe a big part?

              GRAHAM
Possibly.

              ANN
Graham, I mean, what do you think
her reaction is going to be if
you contact her?

              GRAHAM
I don't know.

              ANN
Look at you, look at what's
happened to you, look how you've
changed! Don't you think she will
have changed?

              GRAHAM
I don't know. I really would rather
not talk about it.

              ANN
             (has to laugh)
Whoa!! I'm so glad we got that
on tape!! You won't answer a
question about Elizabeth, but I
have to answer all these intimate
questions about my sex life!!
Graham, what do you think she's
going to make of all these
videotapes? Are you going to tell
her about them? I can't imagine
her being too understanding about
that. But since you don't lie
anymore, you'll have to say
something.

              GRAHAM
As I said, I haven't decided what
to do, exactly. Perhaps I won't
do anything.

                 (CONTINUED)

51   (CONTINUED) (15)   51

                        ANN
              Oh, you just moved here to <u>think</u>
              about it, right?

Graham says nothing. Ann looks at him.

                        ANN
              Oh, God, Graham, this is
              so...pathetic. You´re not even
              what you pretend to be, you´re
              a lie, you´re a bigger lie than
              you ever were.

Graham sets the camera down, thought it continues to record.
He is visibly upset.

                        GRAHAM
              All right, you want to talk about
              lies, let´s talk about lies, Ann.
              Let´s talk about lying to yourself.
              You haven´t been able to sleep
              with your husband because you´re
              no longer in love with him, and
              maybe you never were. You haven´t
              been honest with yourself in longer
              than you can remember.

                        ANN
                    (heated)
              Yeah, you´re right. But I never
              claimed to <u>know</u> everything thing
              like you, and have all these little
              <u>theories</u>. I´m still learning, I
              know that. But I don´t feel like
              I´ve wasted time. If I had to go
              through my marriage to get to where
              I am right now, fine.

Ann moves in closer, burrowing, her eyes on fire.

                        ANN
              But <u>you</u>. You have wasted nine
              <u>years</u>. I mean, that has to be
              some sort of weird record or
              something, nine years. How does
              <u>that</u> feel?

Graham says nothing. Ann picks up the camera and points it at
him.

                        GRAHAM
              Don´t do that.

                                        (CONTINUED)

51   (CONTINUED) (16)   51

                    ANN
          Why not?

                    GRAHAM
          Because.

                    ANN
          "Because"? That´s not good enough.
          I asked you a question, Graham.
          I asked you "how does it feel"?
          How does it feel, Mr. I Want To
          Go Down On You But I Can´t? Do
          you know how many people you´ve
          sucked into your weird little
          world? Including me? Come on,
          how does it feel?

                    GRAHAM
          I can´t tell you like this.

                    ANN
          I´m just going to keep asking until
          you answer. I´m sure there´s plenty
          of tape.

                    GRAHAM
          I don´t find this "turning the
          tables" thing very interesting--

                    ANN
          I don´t care.

Graham reaches up for the camera. Ann knocks his hand away.

                    ANN
          Not until I get some answers. Tell
          what you feel. Not what you <u>think</u>,
          I´ve heard plenty of that. What
          you <u>feel</u>.

Graham is on the verge of completely falling apart.

                    ANN
          Come on!!

                    GRAHAM
          All right!! All right!! You want
          to know? You want to know how
          I feel? I feel ashamed. Is that
          what you wanted to hear?

A pause. Graham regains his composure somewhat.

                              (CONTINUED)

51   (CONTINUED) (17)   51

                         ANN
          Why are you ashamed?

                         GRAHAM
          Jesus Christ, Ann. Why is anybody
          anything? I think you have this
          idea that people are either all
          good or all bad, and you don´t
          allow for any grey areas, and
          that´s what most of us consist
          of.

                         ANN
          You´re not answering me.

                         GRAHAM
               (heated)
          Well, what kind of answer are you
          looking for, Ann? What is it
          exactly that you want to know?

                         ANN
          I want to know why you are the
          way you are!

                         GRAHAM
          And I´m telling you it´s not any
          one thing that I can point to and
          say "That´s why!" It doesn´t work
          that way with people who have
          problems, Ann, it´s not that neat,
          it´s not that tidy! It´s not a
          series of little boxes that you
          can line up and count. Things
          just don´t happen that way.

                         ANN
          But why can´t you just put it all
          behind you? Can´t you just forget
          it? All that stuff you did?

                         GRAHAM
          No, Ann, I can´t. I can´t forget
          it. It´s not something I can fix.
          It´s difficult. There´s something
          in my mind...the way my brain
          works...
               (frustrated)
          God, Ann, when you´re with another
          person, and you´re...inside
                         (more)

                                        (CONTINUED)

51   (CONTINUED) (18)   51

> GRAHAM (Cont´d)
> them, you´re so <u>vulnerable</u>, you´re
> revealing so much...there´s no
> <u>protection</u>. And...somebody could
> say or do something to you while
> you´re in this...state
> of...nakedness. And they could
> hurt you without even knowing it.
> In a way that you couldn´t even
> see.
> (looks at Ann)
> And you would withdraw. To make
> sure it didn´t happen again.

Ann looks at him for a long moment and then sets the camera
down.

She moves in front of Graham and kneels.

> ANN
> I want to touch you.

Graham shakes his head.

> ANN
> I want to touch you.

> GRAHAM
> No.

Ann reaches out, and Graham instinctively begins to move away.

> ANN
> Graham.

Something in her voice makes him stop. Their eyes lock. Graham
slowly moves back toward her.

Ann´s hand eases out to him, her eyes still burning into his.

Graham closes his eyes, accepting Ann´s touch.

She caresses him.

Slowly.

Delicately.

She touches his arms, his face, his hair.

Closing her eyes, she takes his hand and puts it against her
face.

                                        (CONTINUED)

"sex, lies, and videotape"   pg.96

51   (CONTINUED) (19)   51

She begins to lie him back on the couch. When he offers light
resistance, she gently persists.

> ANN
> Keep your eyes closed.

Graham lies back, silently obeying.

Ann touches his face.

Gradually, her hand slips to his neck and she begins to to
unbutton his shirt. She watches his face, hoping that he will
remain calm. He does.

She rubs her hand on his chest.

Once again she brings Graham´s hand to her face. She moves his
hand to her neck and throat, painting her skin with his fingers.

Soon each hand is exploring the other. Fingers search for and
find hidden areas.

Ann stands.

Their hands remain together, and Graham´s eyes remain closed.

Ann moves onto the couch with Graham.

She gently lowers herself into a sitting position on his waist.

She slowly moves both of her hands onto Graham´s chest. They
move forward and back, like a lazy tide.

She looks at Graham. His face is tranquil.

Ann quietly begins to move her face toward his.

Soon she is hovering inches above him, her long hair touching
his features.

She lowers her lips to his forehead and kisses him. She waits
for a negative reaction. Getting none, she moves moves lower
and kisses his eyes. Still receiving no discouragemnt, she moves
to his nose.

A subtle movement from Graham. Ann waits for a moment.

She then moves to his lips, her luxuriant tresses enveloping
his face.

She kisses him lightly.

                                        (CONTINUED)

51 (CONTINUED) (20) 51

She kisses him again.

Graham tilts his head back and she softly kisses his neck.

Graham's hands make their way up Ann's back until they have reached her neck. He slowly pulls his face to hers.

He kisses her.

Graham is flooded with warmth and excitement.

He caresses her, intoxicating himself with physical contact.

The kisses become more meaningful, and the touching becomes more passionate.

For a moment, Graham seems about to evaporate in a state of ecstacy, his eyes filled with relief and happiness.

But his gaze happens to fall on the video camera, which continues to record.

Graham seizes up and abruptly backs away from Ann's embrace.

Reality slowly envelopes him.

               ANN
   Graham...

               GRAHAM
   I'm okay. It's okay.

Ann reaches for his hand. He allows her to take it.

               GRAHAM
      (almost dazed)
   It's okay.

Graham looks at Ann for a long moment. She sees the acceptance and gratitude in his eyes. She smiles lightly.

Graham moves forward and shuts off the camera.

CUT BACK TO:

John watching the tape. There is video snow on the monitor now. The tape timer reads 46:02. John gets up slowly, ejects the tape from the player, and heads for the door.

Graham, hearing the footsteps approach, backs away from the inlet. His eye is swollen, and he holds one of his hands in a curious position.

                      (CONTINUED)

51   (CONTINUED) (21)   51

John opens the door. He looks at Graham for a moment before
reaching into his pocket for Graham´s keys. He dangles them
in his hand as he stands over Graham.

                    JOHN
          I never told you this, because
          I thought it would crush you, but
          now I could give a shit.
                    (pause)
          I fucked Elizabeth. Before you
          broke up. Before you were having
          trouble, even. So you can stop
          making her into a saint. She was
          good in bed and she could keep
          a secret. And that´s about all
          I can say about her.

John drops Graham´s keys to the floor and leaves. Graham stands,
fighting back tears, and walks into his apartment.

He pulls Ann´s tape from the videotape player.

He reaches inside the cassette cartridge and pulls the videotape
itself out, ruining it forever. He does the same to every other
tape in both the boxes. Calmly. Deliberately. Methodically.

He walks over to the camera/recorder, trailing a mound of
videotape behind him. He breaks the lens off the camera body,
and smashes the inner workings against the edge of the table.
He then drops the damaged unit into the pile of destroyed tape,
where it disappears.

CUT TO BLACK:

THEN CUT TO:

52   INT. LAW OFFICES -- DAY   52

John Millaney talks to his colleague.

                    JOHN
          Man, not having to answer to
          anybody... I feel like this huge
          weight has been lifted from my
          shoulders. I mean, come on, if
          I decide that I´d rather live
          alone, what´s so bad about that?
          It´s not like I´ve decided to live
          a life of crime, right?
                    (more)

                                        (CONTINUED)

52   (CONTINUED)   52

                         JOHN (Cont´d)
              It´s just how I feel, you can´t
              help the way you feel, you just
              have to be honest about it.

John dials a number on his telephone.

                         VOICE ON PHONE
              IBM.

                         JOHN
                    (to phone)
              Brian Kirkland, please.

                         VOICE ON PHONE
              May I ask who´s calling?

                         JOHN
              John Millaney.

                         VOICE ON PHONE
              One moment.

                         JOHN
                    (to his colleague)
              Anyway, I´ve always said, the work
              is the thing. I can be happy
              without a marriage, but take away
              my work, that´s different. And
              if Ann can´t handle that, that´s
              <u>her</u> problem, like we´re all alone
              in this world, you know what I´m
              saying? I mean, <u>fuck</u>.
                    (looks at phone)
              Jesus, what´s takin´ this guy?

The intercom clicks to life.

                         SECRETARY
                    (on speaker)
              Mr. Millaney?

                         JOHN
              Yeah.

                         SECRETARY
                    (on speaker)
              Mr. Forman would like to see you
              in his office.

                                        (CONTINUED)

"sex, lies, and videotape"   pg.100

52   (CONTINUED) (2)   52

                         JOHN
              Okay, in a minute, I´m on with
              a client.

                         SECRETARY
                       (on speaker)
              He said <u>immediately</u>.

                         JOHN
              All right, jesus.

The intercom clicks off.

                         VOICE ON PHONE
              Mr. Millaney?

                         JOHN
              Yes?

                         VOICE ON PHONE
              Mr. Kirkland has asked me to inform
              you that he has obtained legal
              representation elsewhere, and that
              if you have a message for him to
              leave it with me.

John swallows.

                         JOHN
              Thank you. I...there is no message.
              Thank you.

John hangs up. He thinks for a moment, rubbing his forehead.

The intercom clicks to life.

                         SECRETARY
                       (on speaker)
              Mr. Millaney, Mr. Forman is
              waiting.

                         DUDE
                       (voice over)
              Come on, I´m not asking too much,
              am I? Just one little question.

53   INT. LOUNGE -- DAY   53

Cynthia is tending bar. The Dude from earlier is still there,
puffing on a big cigar.

                                        (CONTINUED)

"sex, lies, and videotape"   pg.101

53   (CONTINUED)   53

                       DUDE
              Just tell me what time you get
              off. Work, I mean. What's the
              harm in that? Whaddaya say?

Ann enters the lounge. Cynthia watches with apprehensive surprise as Ann approaches with a potted plant.

                       CYNTHIA
                   (to Dude)
              Excuse me.

Cynthia moves to meet Ann at the end of the bar. Ann sets the plant down on the counter. Her manner is diffident, but not hostile.

                       ANN
              I know it's your birthday, and
              I know you like plants. So I got
              you this.

Cynthia is very moved, though she struggles valiantly to conceal her emotions.

                       CYNTHIA
              Thank you.

                       ANN
              Well. I can't stay.

Ann begins to leave.

                       CYNTHIA
              Can I call you?

Ann turns back to face her. They look at each other for a moment.

                       ANN
              Do you have my work number?

                       CYNTHIA
              No.

Ann writes the number down on a napkin.

                       ANN
              I get real busy between two and
              four.

                       CYNTHIA
              Okay.

                                      (CONTINUED)

53   (CONTINUED) (2)   53

Ann looks at Cynthia again before leaving.

> ANN
> Bye.

> CYNTHIA
> Bye.

Ann leaves. Cynthia continues to look at the door long after Ann has left.

> DUDE
> Nice plant.

Cynthia turns to him.

> CYNTHIA
> Do me a favor. Don´t come in here
> anymore.

54   SCENE DELETED   54

55   INT. GRAHAM´S APARTMENT -- DAY   55

Graham sits reading. There is now some furniture in the apartment. Bookshelves, plants, etc. There are periodicals on the table where the video gear used to be. There are no cigarettes.

There is a knock at Graham´s door, which now has a deadbolt lock.

> GRAHAM
> Who is it?

A knock again. Graham sets his book down and goes to the door. He unlocks the deadbolt and opens it.

Ann stands in the hallway.

Graham is obviously flushed with feeling at seeing her. She wordlessly moves into the room, her movements like a slow breeze, her expression calm.

Graham watches her go by.

She stops in the middle of the room, her back to him.

Graham moves toward her slowly. Sensing him behind her, her breathing becomes deep.

> (CONTINUED)

55   (CONTINUED)   55

Graham slowly enfolds her in his arms, his face against her
hair.

She closes her eyes as their fingers entwine.

CUT TO BLACK

THE END

an
outlaw
production

sex, lies, and videotape

written and directed by
STEVEN SODERBERGH

produced by
ROBERT NEWMYER
JOHN HARDY

executive producers
NANCY TENENBAUM
NICK WECHSLER
MORGAN MASON

graham
JAMES SPADER

ann
ANDIE MacDOWELL

john
PETER GALLAGHER

cynthia
LAURA SAN GIACOMO

therapist
RON VAWTER

barfly	STEVEN BRILL
girl on tape	ALEXANDRA ROOT
landlord	EARL T. TAYLOR
john's colleague	DAVID FOIL

photographed by
WALT LLOYD

music by
CLIFF MARTINEZ

casting by
DEBORAH AQUILA

unit production manager	JOHN HARDY
first assistant director	MICHAEL DEMPSEY
script supervisor	ELIZABETH LAMBERT
second assistant director	ALEXANDRA ROOT
production executive	JOHN KAO
art director	JOANNE SCHMIDT
set decorator	VICTORIA SPADER
prop master	AARON GLASCOCK
artwork	AMY ARCHINAL
	BONNIE AMOS
production sound mixer	PAUL LEDFORD
boom operator	STEPHEN TYLER
sound assistant	BEN WILLIAMS
key grip	J.D. STREETT
gaffer	PHIL BEARD
first assistant cameraman	MICHAEL CHARBONNET
second assistant cameraman	TONY BRIGNAC
grips	GILLY CHARBONNET
	JONATHAN CONEY
best boy	DAVID JENSEN
electrician	BUDDY CARR
generator operator	BENNIE ROBERTSON
make-up and costuming	JAMES RYDER
hair stylists	SABRINA LOPEZ
	AMANDA SCHULER
wardrobe	AMANDA MOORE
production coordinators—L.A.	DAVIS GUGGENHEIM
	NANCY McINTOSH
casting assistant	PHILIP JOSTROM
production accountant	BILLY COLLINS, JR.
swing crew chief	BILL CANCIENNE
drivers	ROSS NEILL
	SUSAN BONFILS
production assistants	MELISSA BENEDETTO
	LOUIS KOERNER

catering	RUSTY SMITH
	JIM BRANNON
	Ten/Twenty Caterers
foley	VANESSA AMENT
foley editing	DAVE STONE, M.P.S.E.
foley recording	SCOTT CHANDLER
	Sprocket Systems
dolby stereo consultant	DAVID W. GRAY

sound editing and re-recording
music recording
LARRY BLAKE

picture editing	STEVEN SODERBERGH
post-production	
sound services	Weddington Productions
acoustic guitar music	MARK MANGINI
film-to-tape transfers	Telecine Tech
production consultant	HAROLD WELB
production insurance	The Truman Van Dyke Co.
completion guarantee	ROBERT MINTZ
	The Completion Bond Co.
legal services	HOWARD BEHAR
	HARRIS MILLER
	Wyman Bautzer
	Kuchel & Silbert
film stock	AGFA XT320
negative processing	Allied+WBS Labs, Dallas
negative cutting	STEVE NEW
	SCOTT HILL
	Precision Film Cutting
color timing	DAN MUSCARELLA
prints	CFI

panaflex camera and lenses by panavision
filmed on location in Baton Rouge, Louisiana

29715	(logo) DOLBY STEREO
(MPAA logo)	IN SELECTED THEATRES

MOTION PICTURE ASSOCIATION OF AMERICA

special thanks

ROGER SAVAGE	CHRIS JENKINS
JOHN DUNN	MARK COHEN
SCOTT SAKAMOTO	KEVIN SHINGLETON
STEVE MATHIS	RICHARD ANDERSON
MARK MANGINI	STEPHEN FLICK
BILL LEMOINE	JULIANNE NACHTRAB
SONNY AND ANDREA	ANNE HUMPHREYS
ROGER GUSSINGER	LAURA GUSSINGER
TOM KOBAYASHI	FRANK DUVIC

Shades of the Past Antiques
Le Garage
Sadie Mae's

this film is dedicated to
ANN DOLLARD
1956–1988

during

Here I'm pretending to be in conference with Jimmy so John Hardy won't come over and tell me to stop shooting so much.

1 AUG 88

7 A.M. call for first day of shooting. We did easy stuff today, Jimmy arriving at Ray's Bait Shop, shaving, getting dressed, etc. Good way to start. The most nerve-wracking event of the day occurred when John Hardy handed me a telegram, which I immediately assumed was from the bond company, shutting us down. It was from Larry, Mark, and Annette, wishing me well in Hollywoodese.

Spader said I shoot like an editor, which made sense. All in all, I think this will be a lot easier than making a short, because on shorts (mine, anyway), you end up doing twenty jobs at once. Here I can just concentrate on the performances and camera placement.

The dailies situation will be a little weird. I'll be cutting the film on videotape, so I'm not striking a 35mm mag track since we'll begin syncing the original ¼" audio with the negative during tape transfer at Telecine Tech in Hollywood. Basically that means we'll be watching silent workprint projected onto a cyclorama with an old projector. Sound dailies on videotape will arrive a week to ten days later. Not much room for error.

Well, I think today went very well. 29 to go.

2–3 AUG 88

Good news and bad news.

Bad news. The Bayou bar, where we were shooting, has literally

177

no ventilation, so it was upwards of 110 degrees when we were shooting with the door shut. The lighting rig for the long master shot I requested took a long time to rig because we have a small crew. Three moving actors and a fourth on the telephone combined with six or seven neon signs were giving Paul Ledford stomach ulcers. The two bar scenes (nos. 32 and 53), which were scheduled to be shot in one day, took two, meaning that I was 100% over schedule after the second day of shooting.

Good news. The performances were great. Steve Brill was hysterical. I just told him to flirt, and he just made everything up as he went. Every take had something funny in it. Elizabeth Lambert, my script supervisor, made sure I knew that none of his dialogue really matched from angle to angle. I, of course, told her not to worry, intoxicated as I was with the fact that we were getting good stuff. This will haunt me, I'm sure.

Andie and Laura are wonderful as well. If it's difficult for them to shoot out of sequence, they aren't showing it. Andie added a great little ditty; when Laura says the line about their mom having spotted shoulders and varicose veins, Andie says "Well, Missy Thing, so will you someday." "Missy Thing"! I think Andie said her aunt or somebody would call her that whenever she was putting on airs. Too funny.

More good news. We will shoot all of John's law office stuff on Saturday, instead of Friday/Saturday, meaning we'll be back on schedule by week's end.

Bob was here today. He looked around, sat to Steve Brill's right with a cigarette in scene 32, pronounced that everything looked under control, and left to go back to Los Angeles. I love producers.

4–5 AUG 88

All of Ann's therapy scenes. This was make-or-break stuff. There's a fine line that Andie had to walk between playing someone who is not very self-aware and someone who is outright stupid. Andie nailed it on every take, and Ron was wonderfully insinuating as the therapist. I ended up shooting and printing a lot, but I felt like this was very important stuff, and since I can't go back and reshoot anything, I wanted to make sure (freshman paranoia, I think).

During the scene where Andie says she wants to leave therapy (no. 20), Ron did a great job of putting her in this little trance. It was really creepy.

After Thursday's shooting was completed, Andie asked me if she could talk to me in her trailer. I said of course. I imagined she would say this:

ANDIE: I have to tell you that your breath stinks and I hate the very sound of your voice, so if you must give me direction, please give it to an intermediary and have that person give it to me. You can go now.

ME: Okay.

Of course, nothing in Andie's behavior hinted at such a revelation, and what she actually wanted to tell me was that she just found out that she was pregnant, and she hoped that I wasn't upset. Relieved, I told her that I was very happy for her and Paul (Qualley, her husband), and I hoped she would be okay and to let me know what I can do to make sure she's comfortable, physically and otherwise. Whew.

These scenes went great. Ann will be the way into the movie for most people, and the opening scene was crucial. I predict people will be surprised and impressed by her performance.

I'm really sorry that Ron was here for so short a time. I'll have to use him again. I'm hoping I'll get to see him onstage in New York with The Wooster Group sometime.

Walt got an "emergency" phone call from the lab, and he and I immediately assumed the worst. Turned out one of the timers wanted to know the name of "that girl who's playing the bartender." That's a good sign, I think.

6 AUG 88

Peter's law office scenes (nos. 3, 26, 52). We started with John's opening bit where he's talking to his colleague (David Foil) on the phone. Peter suggested spinning the ring, which was a nice little thing to open on. He made some minor changes in the first speech, and responded to the few lines thrown in by David, who I told to just play along, basically. Alex was drafted to play Janet, the voice of Peter's secretary. Peter came up with the idea of giving Laura a plant, having seen Andie give her a plant in the bar sequence, which occurs later in the film but was shot earlier this week. We did eleven takes on the opening pullback because the zoom lens was acting up. We ended up shooting it with a prime lens, meaning we couldn't get as close to the ring as I wanted initially, but the shot ended up fine. Next we shot John getting the phone call from Cynthia. It's a single shot with a little dolly move, and Peter came up with the "family crisis" excuse, which I thought was pretty funny. I printed both takes.

Then we did John's final scene. David Foil came in to be on camera, which was fun (he acted in my last short film), and David Jensen played the voice of Brian Kirkland's assistant (Kirkland, due to the deForrest report, no longer works anywhere specific, because, ironically enough, there is a Brian Kirkland that works at IBM). The dialogue pretty much remained as is, and Peter did three different levels of anger at the end of the scene so that I can choose in the editing how upset I want John to be. David Foil got his big close-up, and everyone went home happy.

More dailies. Andie blushes on cue!! I guess we weren't close enough to see her when we shot it, but boy, she turned crimson when Ron asked her about masturbating. Those present exchanged looks of disbelief (Andie does not want to see dailies. Peter comes pretty often, as does Laura. Jimmy hasn't come yet). I called Andie to tell her how spectacular the stuff looked. She was very pleased, although it sounded like she didn't believe me. She kept saying "Really?"

I did print too much, though.

8 AUG 88

Eight, eight, eighty-eight. We started a week's worth of shooting at the Millaney house (actually Sonny Cranch's house). The first scene we shot was Andie leaving the house distraught after finding the earring. This was tough because Andie has to get this kind of anger and confusion thing going, and so I tried to make sure she had time to get herself ready, and tried not to talk to her too much (I didn't want to say stupid shit like "Think about children going hungry"). It was a long dolly shot, and during one take I tripped over the track as I was following the shot and did a silent somersault onto the pavement and waited for the take to finish. I said "cut" while lying flat on my back, which was a first for me.

Next was Cynthia leaving after her tryst with John. Quick and easy. I loved how Peter started looking through the mail as soon as the door shut. Cold-blooded.

Next was John arriving home to greet Ann, which is shown during the midnight interrogation scene. Dolly and pedestal up, printed take three. Then Walt, Michael Charbonnet, and I rushed off to get a shot of Peter driving for the same sequence (I doubt I'll use the shot, though).

Next were the two phone conversations between Ann and Cynthia (scenes 22, 31). The first we played in the kitchen with Andie chopping vegetables (not Paul Ledford's idea, I can assure you), while the camera does a horror-movie track around and in. My big direction to Andie and Laura was "faster." Oscar-winning direction, folks; just call me if you need pointers.

For the second phone call, we had Andie by the bathtub. Toyed with the idea of having Andie in the tub (with bubbles, of course), but discarded the notion without sharing it with anyone, lest I be thought a fool.

Once again, Andie and Laura were great. Most of my comments had to do with making sure they weren't playing things too big, or getting out of hand with the accents (Andie is from Gaffney, South Carolina, so her accent is quite real, though I still keep an ear on it. Laura is from New Jersey, and has done a remarkable job of not only picking up pronunciation, but rhythm).

9 AUG 88

Today we shot our first sex scene (no. 15). In the script this scene is very straightforward (too much so. Who wrote this piece of shit?). Lucky for us, Sonny Cranch's home has an unusual design flaw (Sonny designed it himself), in that one can actually see into the master bedroom from the front door. We were able to take advantage of this by having Laura enter the front door and the bedroom within a single frame, with a slight dolly back. Then the question became how to reveal John. I wanted him naked, but obviously we couldn't have Little Elvis just laying there for all to see. Peter came up with the idea of having a plant on his genitals. It seemed consistent, since plants had been exchanged previously. A plant was procured, amidst the predictable jokes about itching powder and fire ants, and I gave Peter and Laura a couple of lines to say after she sits on the bed. Laura's creaky leather skirt was neat.

That was the easy stuff. Next came the scene where Andie finds the earring (no. 42). I decided to try something bold, namely that we started wide and moved in and around to reveal Peter and Laura on the bed behind Andie (an externalization of Ann's thoughts, in theory), then pulled around and back out to see that they are no longer on the bed. Technically, it took a while to coordinate, what with cueing Peter and Laura at just the right instant. My direction to Andie was just to lose it completely, and sure enough, in the three complete takes we got, she went around-the-bend nutso. It was truly frightening to watch (and painful). I looked over at Peter and Laura at one point after a take and their faces were ashen. Peter said to me later "Jeez, I mean, I really felt bad." After we all came down from that, we did the stuff of Andie destroying the earring and ripping herself out of John's clothes. I don't know if anybody will understand that they are John's clothes (obviously she does housework in them), but if they don't, fuggit.

Lastly we shot Andie cleaning the house, which provided much comic relief. It was funny and sad the way she was scrubbing the faucet.

Long day. I hate directing sex scenes, I decided. It makes me uncomfortable to ask people to do such intimate things. I feel like turning away. Invariably, instead of "cut" I say "Okay, that's fine." I realize that over and above the fact that I don't think nudity will be required, I don't know that I could ask an actor to take his/her clothes off. If they *offered* and I thought it was appropriate, then *maybe* (right, I can see that happening real soon). I just don't think I could ask, especially someone like Laura, who, as I get to know her better, I realize is giving a real performance. She's not at all like Cynthia, personally. She's very demure and sweet, and I feel very brotherly and protective of her.

The days are long, mostly because I dream about the film when I sleep, so it seems like I never leave work. There I go, complaining again. I think Lawrence Kasdan said it best: It's not hard to direct; it's hard to direct well.

10 AUG 88

Shot the interrogation scene (no. 35) day-for-night. This played pretty much as written, and was actually a lot of fun to shoot, despite the semi-harrowing aspects of the scene. This was due in large part to the fact that Peter kept cracking up (with off-camera help, I'm sorry to say) on the "dipped in shit" line. On another take, the phone rang (someone had forgotten to keep it off the hook) and Peter, in character, answered. He listened for a few seconds, then said "No, there's no John Hardy here," hung up, and continued the scene. Unfortunately, I started laughing and we cut the take.

Everything went great. I encouraged Peter and Andie to overlap their dialogue, even though I knew it would cause editing headaches later (first for me, then for Larry). Having the conversation sound natural is more important to me than saving time and effort in post-production. I think.

Dailies continue to look great. When is something going to go wrong?

11 AUG 88

Today we shot Jimmy's first real scene (no. 10). It was supposed to have been shot on Monday, but Jimmy got sick and we had to shuffle the schedule a little (he would insist that I make it clear that he has never before been responsible for a scheduling change). I'm sure it was a little strange to come into a situation where a certain rhythm has already been established, but, at the risk of sounding methody, since this particular scene was supposed to be kind of awkward and arryhthmic, I think he did great. During rehearsal Jimmy told me there would come a time when Graham would become his and not mine, and that I should be prepared for that. I felt like that transfer had already taken place when Jimmy arrived on the set today, and I was excited by that fact. I'm happy to let the fucker go.

John Hardy is wry, low-key, and unflappable. He would never, for instance, say to me, "Steve, you're shooting and printing too much!! You'll eat up the contingency!!" He would rather sidle up to me after take four of an eight-minute scene and whisper, "I think you should see these numbers," and the numbers would indicate that if I continued at my present rate, I would at least double the allotted budget for film stock, processing, and printing, which is exactly what he did today. I got the point. I really think I'll shoot less as I go. Really.

12 AUG 88

Our first night shoot. The dinner sequence (no. 11). This took a long time to set up, mostly because I asked for a 270-degree dolly in a very small room, and it took J.D. a while to get rid of all the dolly creaks and Paul a while to get the proper balance between the various mikes without encountering phase problems, not to mention the clanging of utensils on dinnerware, which scramble his brain pretty good.

We did a couple of run-throughs, and made some minor dialogue changes. Peter came up with "held private services in the back of the chapel on a weekly basis," which replaced the line about the unicycle.

Jimmy dropped the bonfire line. From Peter again, "serious salt ac-tion" turned into "achieves critical mass with the salt," which was nice, since Peter had established "critical" as one of John's catch-words, and people use it on the set now. I encouraged everyone to overlap and chime in with whatever they felt was appropriate, and this worked to good effect I thought during the section about where to find an apartment. Jimmy and I decided it was better for him to stay seated throughout the scene instead of getting up to assist Ann as the script indicated.

Being the editor and a cost-conscious director, I shot no coverage on the scene. The opening shot I carried until Andie got up (offscreen on this angle). Andie's angle I shot only from the point where she talks about her family until she gets up, at which point I went to the high shot, which will be held for the remainder of the scene. Plus I shot one additional angle of Jimmy's "key" speech, but I think the opening angle will work better. John Hardy was a happy man, and so was I. Now let's see if it cuts together.

13 AUG 88

Another night shoot. Scenes 48, 12.

For the argument scene, pre-film rehearsals quickly showed that Peter should not actually hit Andie, and I incorporated this into the final draft (John hits Ann in the earlier drafts). There was no doubt that the character of John was capable of such violence, it just seemed unnecessary and possibly misogynist. Peter's idea during rehearsal was to hit everything *but* her, which we modified on the set to him wanting to hit her but not going through with it.

I cut a few lines here and there, and added Andie's " 'Why?' You're asking me 'why?' " Peter came up with "Well, I'm married to you, you want out of this marriage, I think you can tell me that," which led into the all-important "Fuck you." After Andie told Peter about going to Graham's, Peter made up some funny stuff about Gra-ham, like "the Apostle of truth" etc. At one point he came up with "What's the guy want, his own talk show?" but it came out so funny that it pulled you out of the scene. Peter did a great job of exploding, and the scene was palpably intense to watch.

By the time we got upstairs to shoot the scene of Ann watching Graham sleep, Andie was giddy from lack of sleep. She literally was taking weird little bunny-like steps during one take, and I had to walk over to her laughing and say, "Andie, what are you doing?" We eventually got everything we needed and we started wrapping this location. I think we managed not to damage Sonny's house too much. I felt terrible earlier this evening when Sonny and Andrea returned from vacation with the kids and asked if they could watch us film a scene, and I had to say no because I didn't think their kids should see Peter yelling and screaming and saying, "Well, at least you didn't fuck him." So I had to keep them outside. Neither Sonny nor Andrea have read the script yet, so they have no idea what we shot. This is a good thing.

Two weeks down, three to go. On schedule and on budget, according to John Hardy and Billy Collins, Jr. They call the bond company every night with the production report, and the bond person takes the call and every night says, "Okay." Ever since we started shooting it's like they've forgotten about us. I guess they know that once things start rolling you just have to hope for the best. I'm not complaining, I just thought we'd get hassled more, that's all.

14 AUG 88

Day off felt good. Walt, David Foil, and I saw *Tucker: The Man and His Dream*, which we had been dying to see. Unfortunately, I was engaged aesthetically but not emotionally. But there was an endless parade of boner-inducing images. It literally was one of the best designed and photographed films I've ever seen. Loved those cars, too.

15 AUG 88

Cynthia's apartment. After we decided on this particular location, John Hardy went to the owner, who had been told earlier that the title of the film was *Lies and Videotape,* and asked them to sign the rental and insurance agreement. Well, the owner looked at the contract, then up at John Hardy, and said, "Says here sex, *lies, and videotape.*" John then broke into a soft-shoe, stammering "I know it really looks like we're trying to put something over on you . . ." He ultimately convinced the owner that the film is nonpornographic.

First we shot a couple of exteriors, Peter arriving and leaving (scenes 38 and 6). Inside we shot Peter arriving for the first time (scene 6 continued), which plays under Andie's therapy dialogue. Again, I find this stuff difficult, this directing sexual stuff. I ended up saying shit like, "Okay, you give her the plant, then follow her over, and, oh, take off your jacket, yeah, then caress her from behind . . ." I told Laura to drop her necklace after Peter grabs her, but beyond that I said to just go with

whatever felt right (my standard line). Walt decided (and I agreed) that
Cynthia's bedroom should be lit perpetually warm, color-wise. Joanne
and Vicki did a great job with dressing the apartment. When I first
walked in this morning it reminded me so much of the apartment of
the girl that this character is loosely based on that I had *deja vu*. Really,
it was uncanny. It was Joanne's idea that Cynthia be an aspiring artist,
and that was a great notion. It adds a whole dimension to her character
without anything having to be said. The place feels like Cynthia lives
there, which I think is wonderful. I would imagine it helps Laura as
well.

Peter is wearing my Movado watch as part of John's wardrobe.
The Movado was something I had wanted for a long time, and when
I got my first real writing assignment (for Tri-Star in '86), it was the
first thing I bought.

Next was the Cynthia/John postcoital scene (no. 8). With some
very minor exceptions, this remained pretty much as written, but I
don't think there's any way to describe on paper the way Laura moved
down to the edge of the bed and played the last half of the scene
upside-down. Just looking through my cheesy video monitor I could
tell this would be one of my favorite images from the film.

Last shot of the day is Laura getting the first phone call from
Peter (scene 13). Afterward, Paul got some silent room tone to help
Larry in sound editing. You'd be amazed at how difficult it is to get
everyone to shut up for two minutes.

16 AUG 88

We shot the scene where Ann and Cynthia discuss Graham at
Cynthia's apartment (scene no. 19). This, to me, is an example of a
scene that, while remaining very close to what was written, really
came to life when we started blocking (assuming it *did* come to life).
We decided to start it in Cynthia's bedroom, where Ann is sitting on
the edge of the bed (she would never actually sit or lie on Cynthia's
bed, we felt), and when Laura blew cigarette smoke toward Andie at
the beginning of the scene, that propelled Andie to move out of the
bedroom. I then told Andie to explore and Laura to begin dressing for
work, and they both did, with little further input from me. Andie
instinctively returned to the bedroom when the issue of Cynthia visiting Graham required more direct handling, and she also put out
Cynthia's cigarette, which was great (prompting Laura to ad-lib
"Thank you, I was still smoking that," which I loved). The scene was

1. *Rigging the road P.O.V. shot. Tracy Langan at Panavision will have a heart attack when he sees this.*

2. *Ron Vawter does his Rodney Dangerfield impression. I left his best scene (no. 20) on the cutting room floor, although it will appear on a special Criterion CAV laserdisc.*

IPM01LA
4-012712S213 07/31/88
ICS IPMPNGZ CSP
ZCZC 8185068762 FRE TDEN STUDIO CITY CA 64 07-31 0926P EST
PMS STEVEN SODERBERGH, DLR

BT

FOR IMMEDIATE RELEASE: INDUSTRY PUNDITS PREDICTING BOFFO B.O. FOR
FROSH HELMSMAN S A SODERBERGH'S INDIE PRIDE PROD PIX COMMENCING
LENSING TODAY IN STIX. OUR SPY SEZ MUCHO HOOPLA AMIDST RUMORS
INVESTORS THREATENING TO ANKLE FLICK DUE TO DIRECTOR'S LAGGING TWO
DAYS BEHIND SCHEDULE 3 HOURS INTO SHOOTING. FILM'S CHEVY WRANGLER AND
SOCAL TRANSPLANT AARON GLASCOCK QUOTED OFF THE RECORD SEZ "HE
COULDN'T DIRECT TRAFFIC."

CHAMPAGNE WISHES AND CAVIER DREAMS

ANNETTE MARK AND LARRY

NNNN
2127 EST

IPM01LA

3. *The telegram I received on the first day of shooting.*

4. Shooting in The Bayou bar. In an attempt to appear dashing, I wore a starched white shirt for our first indoor shooting with female cast members. Ten minutes after shooting in 110-degree heat I smelled like a moldy dry cleaning store.

5. Second (unscheduled) day of shooting at The Bayou. Andie is apparently mesmerized by a blemish on my chin. Notice I've switched to more sensible clothing.

6. *Shooting the argument scene (no. 48). Peter and I are trying to remember who won the '83 World Series.*

7. *Again, shooting scene 48. Peter and Andie chat between takes. I know they're talking about me.*

8. *I've just stripped in front of the camera to prove to the cast that I'm willing to do nudity if they are. First A.C. Michael Charbonnet is impressed. Andie is not.*

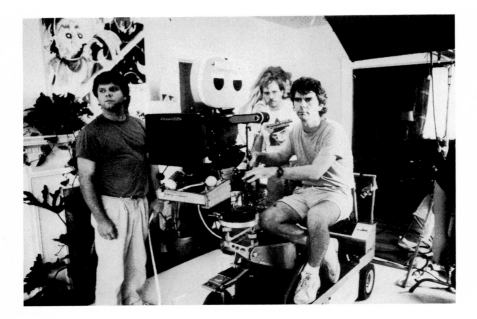

9. *Michael Charbonnet, key grip J.D. Streett, and Walt line up a shot from scene 41. I'm probably just about to turn to them and say, "Are you waiting on me?"*

10. *Jimmy with the ever-present iced tea in scene 24. The only faces on the wall behind him that I recognize are Lillian Gish and J. Robert Oppenheimer. I should have asked Joanne Schmidt and Vicki Spader who they all were so I could give interviews about their significance.*

11. *Laura from scene 24. She played this scene just right, I think. I was afraid people wouldn't buy that Cynthia would just show up at Graham's, but Laura made it believable. Behind her is the map with all the routes Jimmy has driven by car.*

12. *An action shot!! Just below frame is the air cannon used to catapult Jimmy to his feet.*

13. *John Hardy and I doing what we do best: watching people work. I look like I'm about to spit. John looks happy because we're nearing the end of shooting.*

14. The key image from the film, in my opinion. I wanted to use this on the poster. The only people who agreed were the German distributors.

15. Shooting the fight sequence. Jimmy got to have this really cool blood squib in his mouth, just like James Caan in The Godfather!

16. *This was an image used in some early campaigns, like the American Film Market in February '89. I thought this would look great on a poster as well. Only the Japanese distributor agreed.*

17. *Groveling and foot-kissing seemed to work well on the female cast members. The males, inexplicably, did not respond as well.*

SND. ROLL

PLEASE PLACE 15 ft. OF BLACK
BEFORE FIRST SHOT

event #	edge # IN	+FR	edge # OUT	+FR	time code # IN	time code # OUT	sc.	tk.	notes
MOS	F576445	00	F576469	15	15:35:39:29	15:35:56:19	R1M	1	DRIVING P.O.V.
"	F576470	03	F576478	02	15:35:56:24	15:36:02:02	R1M	1	" "
"	F576479	11	F576481	07	15:36:03:04	15:36:04:09	R1M	1	" "
"	F445779	13+	F445784	02	11:54:03:16	11:54:06:12	1K	1	GRAHAM DRIVING
"	F576485	04-	F576489	11	15:36:06:26	15:36:09:24	R1M	1	DRIVING P.O.V.
"	F576491	15	F576509	02+	15:36:11:09	15:36:22:23	R1M	1	" "
1	F245647	00-	F245661	07	08:41:08:09	08:41:17:27	1	4	EXT. RAY'S
1	F245877	02-	F245892	05	10:28:21:21	10:28:31:24	1C	1	GRAHAM ENTERS
14	F812362	15-	F812386	00	11:57:45:24	11:58:01:04	2A	3	ANN C.U.
1	F246259	01	F246271	09	11:15:48:06	11:15:56:15	1D	1	GRAHAM SHAVING
11	F597457	10+	F597495	08-	10:13:03:24	10:13:29:01	2	2	ANN & DOC; WIDE
2	F606178	02	F606215	10	11:45:36:17	11:46:01:17	1E	3	GRAHAM CHANGES
13	F236433	00+	F236489	06+	11:44:17:11	11:44:54:29	2A	2	ANN C.U.
25	F143261	10	F143342	12-	11:23:02:21	11:23:56:23	3	11	JOHN IN OFFICE
25	F143751	03-	F143797	03-	12:37:37:06	12:38:07:25	3B	2	JOHN; REVERSE ANG

18. Page 1 of 42 pages worth of hand-rendered editing logs.

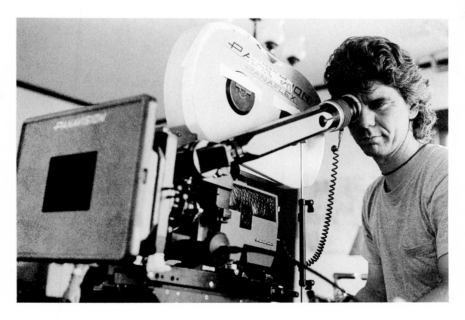

19. Walt Lloyd, the hardest working man in show business now that James Brown is on hiatus. I am jealous of Walt's hair.

20. The "couch scene." Good thing Jimmy and Andie had some ideas, or we'd still be shooting this.

21. *To get the proper expression for this shot, John Hardy and I arranged to have a UFO land just outside the window.*

22. Jimmy preparing to smash one of two perfect replicas built by Aaron Glascock for the destruction scene. He busted them up good, real good!

23. A ticket stub from the first public showing of sex, lies, and videotape.

shot with six set-ups, and we averaged about three takes per angle. I told Andie to play it very small, and she did, although she also told me she doesn't want to seem unemotional. I told her not to worry (classic bullshit director line. At least I haven't said "trust me" to anybody. Yet).

Last shot of the day is Cynthia getting the second phone call from John (scene no. 23), and for this I stole a shot from *Blood Simple,* where the camera follows the feet at floor level (which I'm sure the Coen brothers stole from somewhere else). We had a pan of water just outside of frame for Laura to step out of, in order that she drip properly.

Dailies continue to look great (and sound great. We finally got some synced dailies on tape. Paul is doing a great job, despite the time pressures). Walt is extremely happy with Allied + WBS, saying these are the most consistent dailies he's ever seen. I'm very impressed with this Agfa XT320. The grain is very fine, and the blacks are gorgeous (Walt rates the film at ASA 250 to get a denser negative). Dailies are quite fun, and open to everyone (on the crew). J.D. usually brings his portable CD player, and so we have Steely Dan playing over the footage, or sometimes The Police. I usually arrive first, with either Walt or John Hardy right behind me, and we pull the old rented projector out from the corner, point it at the cyclorama (which is white, fortunately), and set up the few folding chairs that are available. I'm sure Kubrick does this.

James Ryder is doing an amazing job with the make-up. He turned down a job as an assistant on *Steel Magnolias* to be the main man on *sex, lies,* and boy, am I glad he did. He and his crew are working for peanuts in the hopes that this film will help them get work in the future. I think it will.

17 AUG 88

On the way to the set with Walt this morning, I told Walt that I wanted to do a reverse zoom for Cynthia's orgasm shot. He said okay, and word quickly spread amongst the camera crew.

The Big O Shot, as it was referred to, was not an easy one to accomplish, on any level. Technically, it required a great deal of preparation (the floor markings that Michael Charbonnet made up for the focus pulling were beautiful), and all this was complicated by a finicky zoom control (when I moaned about this, Walt explained that this was not unusual, and that on *normal* movies, one would have two

of everything on hand for just such an emergency. Sounded terrifi-
cally unexciting to me). First shot went at around 11:30 A.M.

Emotionally, it was a very tricky scene for Laura. Even though
there was no nudity, in order for us to get the frame line as low as
possible she had her breasts taped, which I'm sure was uncomfortable
in every sense of the word. What do you tell an actor who must
simulate orgasm? "Make it convincing"? In this case I told Laura the
kind of shot it was going to be visually, and that I required very little,
if any, movement from her. I told her to pick a point just above the
camera to focus on. The set was cleared (actually, the set is almost
always cleared, either because of sensitive emotional material or lack
of space), and we shot six takes, Laura improving on each (I printed
1, 5, & 6).

The reverse zoom is a gimmicky shot to be sure, and my desire
to use it here stemmed from a feeling that this particular (brief) scene
(no. 28) required a little stylization. For the second shot of the scene
I put the camera on its side and had it lowering slowly toward the
floor as Laura drops into frame (facilitating the only rack focus shot
in the film as well). The crew likes doing those kinds of shots, that's
for sure.

Having gotten that stuff out of the way, we moved on to simpler
things, technically and emotionally, namely Laura's half of scene 31,
where she is talking to Ann about making the tape with Graham. It
was decided that in the unlikely event somebody might miss the idea
that Ann and Cynthia are *opposites,* we should have Laura doing
something to pound this home. So, since Andie was by the bathtub,
having just *cleaned herself,* we decide to have Laura potting a plant,
or *dirtying herself.* These are secrets, folks, things you could never
figure out on your own. Really, though, I thought it played well, and
it seemed perfectly consistent with the characters. Laura looked great
in her big glasses.

I made a small dialogue change during rehearsal. In the script,
Ann says "Did he touch you?" and Cynthia says "No, but I did." Now,
not only did that response seem potentially confusing, but the whole
point of the scene is that Cynthia wants to make Ann suffer and work
for each piece of information, excited by the knowledge that Ann has
to know what happened but won't admit as much. So I made it this:

ANN

Did he touch you?

CYNTHIA

No.

ANN

Did you touch him?

CYNTHIA

No.

Pause. Ann knows something happened. But what?

ANN

Did anybody touch anybody?

CYNTHIA

Well . . . yes.

Ann puts it together.

ANN

Don't tell me. Don't tell me. You didn't.

CYNTHIA

I did.

*   *   *

Etc., etc. And then we went back to the script. It's a minor change, I admit, but crucial to me, because it seemed to sum up the essence of how Ann and Cynthia communicate (or don't communicate).

18 AUG 88

Scene 41, the last scene between John and Cynthia. Again, as in scene 19, blocking played a big part in making the scene come off the page. It started on the bed (John, as opposed to Ann, is obviously very comfortable on the bed). Then Laura got up off the bed and started taking pictures off the wall in an attempt to rearrange the apartment somewhat. The idea was this (again, are you ready for some secrets?): Cynthia is getting ready to dump John, *knows* that she will dump John, and is also contemplating some overall changes in her life, and taking down what is on the walls is the first (unconscious) indication that this change is occurring. Peter, feeling that John senses this, came up with the idea that John is uncomfortable when things move out of the bedroom, and therefore the observant among you will notice how he squirms every time he sits in a chair until finally he blurts, "Jesus, is there one chair in this place that works?" Again, this was interesting stuff to me as long as it remained unspoken and wasn't executed by the actors or myself in such a way that demanded attention.

Dialogue changes: Peter came up with "I should've known, when he showed up dressed like some undertaker from the art world" and " 'Interact'? Whatever that means." I encouraged them both to overlap during the masturbation stuff. Laura added "No, sir" and the laughing, prompting Peter to do the "It's not funny" bit. Peter also cut Laura off during her "liar" speech and interjected "I know, I know, second lowest form of human being. And the first!" which I thought was hysterical. Peter did a great reaction on the third chair, and I cut Cynthia's line "and I'll see you at your house for a family dinner sometime" since that seemed highly unlikely. Another Cynthia cut: Went directly from "I've just been thinking about things, that's all" to "So just leave." Peter suggested a resigned "Yeah, you're right" to Cynthia's line about them having nothing to talk about, which I liked a lot. The shot at the end of the scene where Peter walks right up to the camera I stole from Sidney Lumet. He often frames people like that, and *Fail Safe* and *The Pawnbroker* both had a big influence on me. Welles used that framing a lot as well, come to think of it. Second-hand theft, once again.

Finished with Cynthia's apartment. I think scenes 19 and 41 may be my favorites so far, although I'll admit to having new favorite scenes every other day. Is this a bad sign?

19 AUG 88

Shot pick-ups today: Jimmy driving up to the Millaney house, walking to the door, etc. I tried not to show the video camera in the trunk too obviously. Ideally, most people wouldn't really see it clearly until the second viewing (will there be a second viewing?).

We then went to shoot Andie walking to The Bayou bar, for the head of scenes 32 and 53. It rained like a motherfucker just as we finished. Short day.

20 AUG 88

Long day. The cafe scene (no. 16), which we shot in very long takes. There were only five set-ups, but before I knew it, the day was gone. Jimmy did the scene a couple of different ways, and so I ended up printing several takes.

I cut the line about having kids. The mere idea of Ann having a child with John was just too scary.

The scene went smoothly, although Paul went crazy with the traffic noise ("Don't worry," I told him) and Elizabeth Lambert made me aware of a myriad of continuity errors involving hand placement ("Don't worry," I told her).

We shot the opening P.O.V. shot of the road, which was fun. It's a little frightening to have a Panaflex suspended off the end of a plank in front of a moving car, though.

3 weeks down. Two to go.

21 AUG 88

Saw *Married to the Mob,* which I thought was . . . I don't know. I'm a big fan of Jonathan Demme (during high school I literally watched *Handle With Care* a dozen times inside a week on cable) and there was a lot to like in this movie, I just . . . have to see it again, I think. I remember in 1980 seeing *Raging Bull* three times, and only after the third time did I realize what a great film it was. I'm just slow, I guess.

22 AUG 88

We started two weeks' worth of filming at Graham's apartment with something simple—Andie getting out of her car (scene 44). Actually, we're using Walt's rental car as Ann's picture vehicle. Saves money, and hey, it's already insured (Walt has threatened on occasion to show me his brake turn). I find scenes without dialogue more difficult to direct than scenes with dialogue. In scenes without dialogue, I end up saying stupid shit like, "Keep your mouth half-open until you open the door." I don't know, it just seems weird.

Next was scene 21, where Ann drops in on Graham. Several things have been decided upon by me, Jimmy, Joanne Schmidt, and Vicki Spader for Graham's apartment. Firstly, the furniture, such as it is, will be in different places for each scene. Secondly, the pictures of different faces on the wall(s) will increase in number and change location slightly. Different windows will be covered with different sheets depending upon Walt's needs and desires for each scene. The Xerox copies of the faces were made by Joanne and Vicki, and I have no idea who many of them are. I'm already anticipating that someone will inject these pictures with "meaning." Shit, maybe they do mean something. Jimmy has put a map on the wall (the map will also move) that has Magic Marker lines for every route Jimmy has actually driven in the U.S. Impressive.

So we did the wide shot of Jimmy getting out of the chair and Andie coming in, with only one line change: "Nothing I can't finish later" became simply "I can finish later." A cheap laugh no matter how it's said, let's face it. Then we shot the angle of Jimmy going into the kitchen and a little of his return when it started to rain like crazy, so instead of doing the turnaround for Andie's stuff, I decided to shoot the Girl on Tape video material off the monitor. As for who played the Girl on Tape, Jennifer Jason Leigh tried to do what was required with her boyfriend acting as cameraman, but she was unhappy with the results and called me at the end of last week, very apologetic, saying it just didn't work out. I understood, since it was kind of a tough thing to do with no direct guidance. Plus, she's about to start *Last Exit to Brooklyn,* so I doubt she's spending all of her time thinking about her possible cameo in *sex, lies.* So, as of this weekend, I still didn't have a Girl on Tape. Well, I figured since Alex had successfully dealt with every responsibility thrown her way, I should ask her to be the Girl on Tape (and she was right there in the apartment!). Under threat of dismissal she agreed, and last night Alex, Aaron, and I sat in the apartment and thought up some questions and basic answers (I didn't want to work from a rigid script). Alex also called some of her girlfriends in Los Angeles to get additional material. Eventually, I turned on the camera, did my very best Spader impression, and prompted Alex into telling some stories. We taped for about thirty minutes, and she did an amazing job. She sounded completely like herself. In the end, Alex said she didn't know what her mom would think, but a day's worth of scale acting pay was a nice bonus on top of the slave wages she's getting (and think of the experience and knowledge she's getting, right?). I really lucked out this time.

So we shot the Girl on Tape stuff and a few appropriate inserts. We distressed the video a little to make it more . . . video-like, I guess. 8mm video actually looks quite good. We couldn't afford the expensive film/video synchronizer or 24-frame video, so we got the poor man's synchronizer, which eliminates the roll bar but still leaves a flicker of sorts. Walt and I like the flicker, John Hardy doesn't. Guess we outvoted him on that one.

We'll have to finish the rest of scene 21 tomorrow. I hate splitting scenes up like that. I always figure nothing will match. More neophyte paranoia.

23 AUG 88

We started with Jimmy's angle of scene 21 where he returns with Ann's iced tea (Jimmy's idea, both the getting of something to drink and the fact that it should be iced tea). Everything went great (I especially liked Jimmy's reaction as Ann leaves), and we did the turnaround to get Andie's stuff. During a run-through, Andie came up with a great bit where she was oblivious to the fact that she was spilling her tea. It turned out to be my favorite thing in the scene. My only real direction to her was that while Jimmy is explaining what the tapes are, she should be looking for ways to get out of the apartment, literally. Windows, doors, just flash on how to get away, I told her. She did it beautifully. It was sad, in a way. The character's response, I mean. She's truly confused and upset (words Graham will use to describe her in a later scene).

Next we started scene 24, which is Cynthia's arrival. I decided, despite the very real possibility of boring the audience stiff, to use very few angles in this scene (only two, in fact, up to the point where Laura goes to look at the tapes).

First we did Jimmy's angle (I realize now that there is an unspoken hierarchy about who gets their angles first. On this show it's Jimmy. He didn't ask for it, that's just the way it's turned out). We did seven takes of the first four minutes (stopping where he rises from his chair to follow Laura), and I sensed that Jimmy was not happy and that I probably wasn't helping because I was tending to like everything he was doing. We were starting to be pressed for time, and Jimmy asked if he could do the first half of the scene again, up to the point where he returns with the iced tea (a recurring motif now). I agreed and we shot one more, which I printed. We did a quick turnaround and got Laura's equivalent angle in three takes.

I felt there were several reasons why Jimmy wasn't entirely pleased. One of them was the fact that since the scene required a decent amount of focus pulling, we sometimes had to bust a take or call it NG if Walt or Michael Charbonnet felt it wasn't right. It was also the first time (and I hope, though it doesn't seem possible, the last) that

I had to say to an actor "I don't know if we have time to do it again."

At the end of the day Jimmy and I talked and he expressed his feelings about the day and I expressed mine and everything was very calm. Ultimately, he's just concerned with giving a good performance, which I obviously understand and appreciate. Graham is a very ambiguous character, a dissembler, and Jimmy is just trying to get it right.

Back at the production office after today's shooting, John Hardy and Michael Dempsey talked to me about how the day went and what the schedule looks like. The ultimate thrust of the conversation was that I'll have to move a little faster, and their suggestion is for me to spend more time before and between set-ups with the actors, especially Jimmy. They feel that a lot of the discussions Jimmy and I have could take place while the crew is setting up, and they honestly think he responds to me and I should use that to help move things along. I agreed to spend more time in the actors' trailers (small trailers, don't worry). I would've hung out there more before, except I felt guilty sitting in a comfortable, air-conditioned trailer while Walt and twenty other people sweated to make sure my words got up on the screen. But the performances are the priority, and since we're in the "critical" phase, I have to use my time where it has the most benefit.

24 AUG 88

What a difference a day makes. We got an enormous amount of work done today. We finished scene 24, which remained pretty much as written (Jimmy and Laura rounded out a few things), then we shot the contents of Cynthia's tape, which I don't think was easy for Laura. It's a scene of incredible vulnerability, and I just felt like I didn't want her to do it too many times (we did two).

Then we turned around, shot Jimmy's angles on the second half of 24, and also shot him watching the Girl on Tape (the opening of scene 21), and Cynthia's tape (scene 27). Jimmy can go without blinking longer than any non-amphibian I've ever seen. He did some great reactions. When he heard Ann's knocking, he looked like he was coming out of hypnosis. The reaction to the Cynthia tape was good, also. I wanted it to be clear that Graham is no longer deriving pleasure from the tapes.

Spending quality time with Jimmy had a direct benefit. We never did more than four takes today, and yet we were both much happier than yesterday. That is because we talked more, and had a better idea of what needed to take place. Laura, as usual, was her own great self. She really pulled off the taping stuff well. I didn't want it to be lurid or off-putting, and she made it seem natural. She wasn't ashamed. That's very important. Cynthia is not ashamed of what she does, even if she ends up doing something wrong. The look on Laura's face through the screen door (scene 25) was perfect. It was wistful some- how, and vaguely melancholy. I'm a sucker for both.

25 AUG 88

First we shot the Cynthia video off the monitor.

Then we shot scene 34. Now, I must say, I'm having trouble with this scene, because I don't think I believe it. I think it's a tough sell, asking people to buy that Cynthia would come back to make another tape. The fact that she's "asking for it" makes me uncomfortable. Why have the scene? Well, the main point is to show that Graham isn't really into this taping thing so much anymore. We set it up and did it, and the actors were fine, but it was the first time I didn't care for what I was seeing. I don't know, maybe it'll be great when it's cut together.

This was Laura's last scene on the movie. I'll miss having her around. We taught her a few trick phrases to say on the set of her next film, like "Could you throw some opal on the 5K?" and "Checking the gate" after a printed take. I'm very proud that this was her first feature film.

Walt, John Hardy, and I then spent a decent amount of time scheduling the upcoming portion of the shoot in detail. There are many cinematic time shifts and certain things need to be on tape for later scenes that actually occurred earlier, etc. At times it seemed like a movie version of an Escher drawing, but we got it figured out.

The first thing we had to shoot was the portion of Ann's tape that we see on the monitor. We did the blocking, then I operated the video camera with Jimmy right behind me. I was especially impressed by Andie's concentration during this process. Then we worked on the next section a little bit, where we go into the videotape on film (I know that seems confusing). We stopped to get the day's last two shots: scenes 46 and 50. 46 was easy, your basic dusk shot. 50 was interest- ing. For the "fight" sequence, Walt and I decided to go hand-held for the only time in the film, and this will start with Peter getting out of the car (which belongs to John Hardy. Saving money, once again, although I have to believe if John had anticipated how Peter was going to approach at fifty-five miles an hour and slam on the brakes each time he would have rented a picture car. Or painted Walt's a different color). Despite the fact that the Panaflex is very well designed for hand-held, I could tell it was still quite heavy, especially when one is running and stopping abruptly. Walt's really been killing himself on this film. Most everyone on the show had only done commercial work, where traditionally there is more time to shoot less footage. Walt has had to push the crew hard, and they have responded. Walt is a strong but fair leader, and everyone respects him and his work, especially me. One day he made a suggestion for something and asked if I had a problem with it, and I said "No, I love having my authority undermined." Walt, thinking I was serious, was crushed. I had to speak with him later and make sure he understood that I was joking, the poor guy. He understands my sense of humor better now. I think.

26 AUG 88

Night shoot. Fight scene. It was painfully obvious during the blocking that for John and Graham to have any sort of dialogue here was stupid. We decided that Peter should just come in the door ("It's open," as Graham has told us), start looking for the tapes, and belt Jimmy as soon as possible. It took a few moments to get the punch worked out (no stunt coordinator, of course), but the actual shooting went great. It was literally scary to be so close to it while it was happening. It had all the awkwardness of spontaneous violence. Jimmy took the punch so well I had to wonder if he'd been belted in the jaw his whole life.

Next were Peter's reactions to watching the tape and various shots of Ann's videotape on the monitor.

Tonight was a good indication of the difference in working styles between actors, in this case Jimmy and Peter. When we started blocking the fight scene and all of us knew that dialogue was unnecessary, Jimmy laid out the reasons why (all of which were true), whereas Peter listened to the discussion and said "Why don't I just come in and clock him one?" Obviously, they both went after the same result in different directions. It was funny to watch. Every actor has a different way of preparing, and an audience doesn't care what method or technique is used or isn't used, they just want results. My feeling is "whatever works."

27 AUG 88

Long night. We started with exterior shots of Jimmy being thrown and locked out of the apartment (again, Jimmy is incredibly convincing. I've given up trying to figure out why), ending with Peter coming out after having seen Ann's tape. Peter did a great job with the scene, and that being his last shot on the film, there were many heartfelt good-byes. I feel like he enjoyed himself, which is important to me. I want the actors to feel like they were given the opportunity to give their best. At the risk of sounding like a granola-head, it seemed like invisible hands got Peter this role, and I am incredibly thankful.

We then went inside to shoot Jimmy destroying the tapes. This was difficult only because Jimmy, I think, would have preferred to play it in one shot, and I, wanting to cover myself, wanted to shoot a lot of coverage. Watching Jimmy destroy two boxes of tapes and bloody his hands on the master shot was undeniably powerful, but I had the feeling that was partially due to the fact that we were being pelted by thrown cassettes. Jimmy gladly agreed to do all of the various inserts I requested (and there were quite a few).

Tonight was an example of the cinematographer's dilemma. Walt said he always has a terrible time with job interviews because he is invariably asked two questions: "What is your style?" (to which Walt replies "I don't know until I've read the script") and "How many set-ups a day do you shoot?" (to which Walt replies "It depends"). Most producers, unhappy with Walt's responses, think "That guy doesn't know what he's talking about." Tonight we shot 21 set-ups, which is pretty high for shooting night interiors and exteriors with a single camera. But we only covered 1½ pages of script. On the night we shot the dinner sequence we shot four set-ups, which is low by any standards. But we shot 4¼ pages, which is high. Both days were successful shooting days. So Walt (and others as honest and talented) has to struggle with questions that have no easy answers, and the answers that are available often depend on other people (the director, usually). Oh well, *I'll* hire him.

28 AUG 88

Sleep. Nancy T. and Morgan arrived today. Morgan will be here for a day, and Nancy will stay through the end of shooting. They both exhibited infectious good spirits.

29 AUG 88

Today we shot the pre-taping sequence (scene 45), where Ann, having driven to Graham's apartment, tells him she knows about John, and eventually asks to make a tape. Everything went fine, dialogue remaining essentially as is (Jimmy offered water to Andie, explaining that he was out of iced tea). Andie's angles will be a problem in post because of torrential rain, which screwed us audio-wise. I kept telling Andie to keep things small, and I think she still worries that she's not doing anything. I can see that she is. If she is comfortable she can be amazingly unself-conscious in front of the camera, so I do everything I can to make sure she's comfortable. I don't have to tell Jimmy that much anymore, except when I see something I have a problem with, which isn't often.

Jimmy came up with the line "Under my mattress," replacing "I have money" as the response to Ann's query about where his money comes from. In an early draft, Graham explained that he had been in a car accident and received a settlement, but I felt like why go into that now. Hence the admittedly glib reply.

After we finished scene 45, Walt and I worked out a visual plan for the remaining Ann and Graham section of scene 51 ("inside" the tape). We stopped at the point where Andie picks up the camera. Up to that point, we broke the scene into three sections, which will be divided by two inserts of the video camera.

30 AUG 88

Today we did sections 1 & 2 of the taping scene (from the point where we go inside the tape to where Ann asks Graham "Are you still like that?" and he says no). We shot a few more takes than usual (around six) but that's because we're getting into the marrow of the film, and we have to nail it. Today went well, even though I had my Most Embarrassing Moment as a Director. We were shooting where the camera comes from behind Andie to reveal Jimmy, and to warm into it, Jimmy and Andie were starting the scene with the line "Have you ever thought about having sex with someone other than your husband?" So we were shooting, and Jimmy says, *as it appears in the script,* "Why don't we stop?" At that point I stood up and said "Okay, cut it" and everyone turned to look at me. I looked at everyone, and they started laughing. I tried to explain that I obviously thought Jimmy was serious, but when you've written the thing yourself, it *is* a weak excuse. I am sure this never happened to Preston Sturges.

We did a retake of the road P.O.V. diving board shot because the previous attempt had a water spot on the lens.

31 AUG 88

A good day. We started with section 3 (from "So you're never going to make love again?" to where Andie picks up the camera), doing a turnaround from section 2 and executing matching 180-degree dollies around Jimmy and Andie, which contained some delicate and hopefully revelatory dialogue. The toughest thing has been the dropping of the whole "Elizabeth" shoe, which I think Jimmy handled remarkably, given the material at hand. This is the one aspect of the script that has always bothered me, and I've never been able to deal with it to anybody's satisfaction (witness the shameful retarded child draft/attempt. Talk about blackmail material . . .). Right now I think it's as good as I could make it, but I don't think Robert Towne is losing sleep.

We shot up to the point where Andie picks up the camera and forces Jimmy into the living room. I know that Jimmy and I feel the upcoming section of the scene needs a lot of dialogue work. I'll think on it tonight.

1 SEP 88

We spent the whole day shooting from where Jimmy crosses into the living room to where Ann is about to approach him on the couch.

First, Jimmy and I marked all the dialogue we didn't like, which was some of page 90 and all of 91, basically. Jimmy hated the "two-stepping" line, and the stuff that followed was too succinct. Jimmy proffered "What? What do you want me to tell you? Ann, you don't have the slightest idea who I am," and I followed with "Should I recount all the events in my life leading up to this moment and just hope that it's coherent, that it makes some sort of sense to you?" Jimmy then added "It doesn't make any sense to me. I don't have the slightest idea who I am, and I'm supposed to explain it to you?" Then we went back to the script a little, having Jimmy ask why he should explain himself and Andie responding (the line of Graham's "My problem? Do I have a problem?" was Jimmy's from a pre-film rehearsal). Ann's mini-speech in the middle of page 90 became "You have a problem." Jimmy took "Any problem I might have . . ." and turned it into "You're right. I have a lot of problems. But they belong to me," which I liked. I rewrote Ann's response to this, coming up with:

ANN

You think they're yours, but they're not. Everybody that comes in here becomes part of your problem, everybody that comes in contact with you. I didn't want to be part of your problem, but I am. I'm leaving my husband. Maybe I would have anyway, but the fact is I'm leaving him now, and part of it's because of you. You've had an effect on my life.

Jimmy modified Graham's last lines on page 90 into "This isn't supposed to happen. I've spent nine years structuring my life so that this didn't happen." After this seat-of-the-pants rewriting, all of the dialogue on page 91 seemed stupid, so we just shot the thing. Each take had a little something different so I ended up printing several.

Initially I thought I would have Andie get really big and dramatic for her speech about Graham's problem, but while rehearsing it seemed better played small, for two reasons. One, she's got him pegged and they both know it, so why shout? Secondly, I thought about how the script for me was always about the quiet ways in which people hide and reveal themselves through conversation in little rooms behind closed doors. The whole thing grew out of a "What's going on in the normal-looking house" idea. All the verbal things that have hit me hard in my life have been said quietly. Again, Andie was concerned that she wasn't doing anything, but that's because she couldn't see what I was seeing. It was all there.

I was happy with the changes we made. I thought the ideas were getting across without the feeling that ideas were coming across. Andie's speech really pulled me in. I could feel the change that had taken place in Ann.

At the end of shooting Walt and I rushed over to Sonny Cranch's house to get a dusk shot of the Millaney house for use before the dinner scene.

Tomorrow is the couch scene. I have no idea what will happen.

2 SEP 88

Well, Paul Ledford had a light day (for the first time), since there was no dialogue recording.

When Andie and Jimmy came in this morning, I sent everyone but Walt outside, and we started blocking. At the risk of oversimplifying, we did a lot of "What if I tried *this?*" and "Why don't you do *that?*" until we got what we wanted. This was a situation where you just kind of throw the script away. Stuff like her using his hand to touch her face I wanted to keep because I thought it was erotic, but if I were Jimmy, I'd be wondering how I was going to "evaporate into a state of ecstasy," as the script so impudently requested. At one point, after Graham has kissed Ann, I told Jimmy to let his eyes fall onto the video camera, and noticing that it is still recording, to get up and turn it off. Jimmy had a problem with this, and sensing that this would be an involved discussion, I sent everyone out. He explained that he was fuzzy on why Graham would even notice the camera, much less turn it off, feeling that Graham is so far into another area at this point that his mind wouldn't be so mired in reality. I agreed, but explained that it was very important that Graham, unconsciously or not, not allow the intimacy between himself and Ann to be documented. Graham has finally put the taping thing behind him, I said, and the idea of he and Ann being recorded is now offensive to him. I also explained that logistically I must have someone turn off the camera in order to get back to Peter watching snow on the monitor. Jimmy understood and the discussion ended. I called everyone in and we shot it, going no more than three takes on anything. Though it's hard to judge until the stuff is cut together, I believed what was happening, which is how I judge things (and why scene 34 seemed wrong. It wasn't the actors, I just didn't believe what they were asked to do).

At the end of the day Jimmy came up to me and said he really appreciated my taking the time to talk privately with him about the couch scene. He said the discussion clarified the issue for him, and he was appreciative of the effort on my part. I thought that was very nice.

There was a sense of things coming to an end when the day was over, since tomorrow is the last day, and probably short as well.

3 SEP 88

Last day. We started with the shot of Jimmy getting up to turn off the camera, then let the art department prepare for the last scene (55). As we were moving, Jimmy and Andie approached me and Jimmy said "Can Andie and I tell you about our idea for the last scene?" I said sure, and Jimmy said they'd been talking, and since the whole movie plays indoors (and a lot of it in Graham's apartment), they thought it would be nice to have the last scene outdoors, maybe on the front stairs. I said it sounded fine to me, and went to tell Joanne to strip the apartment bare for the landlord scene (14). She looked happy.

We set up the shot(s) of Andie coming to see Graham on the steps. Jimmy and Andie improvised some dialogue, and on the take that I liked, I can already see people reading significance into Jimmy's line about the rain. It *was* starting to rain, but I doubt you'll see it on film, because it was kind of drizzly, and we weren't backlighting for it.

By the time we finished scene 55 Graham's apartment had been stripped down and prepped for shooting scene 14 with the landlord. Earl T. Taylor, a local actor recommended to me by David Foil, was playing the landlord. We blocked to play the scene in one shot (boy, did we smell pay dirt) and other than the few informational lines that needed to be said, I told Earl to make some stuff up (my favorite: "You'll need a shower curtain, and make sure you put something in the tub so you won't fall"). Three takes and we were done.

Andie recorded some wild lines for scene 51 and we wrapped at 1:33 P.M. and took a cast and crew photo (Jimmy, Andie, and Earl representing the cast).

We exposed 126,150 feet of negative, of which 60,997 feet were printed.

At the wrap party I won the all-male wet T-shirt contest. I want to think it wasn't because I was the director.

after

Mark Mangini, Larry Blake, me, and Aaron Glascock in the multi-track editing/mixing room in North Hollywood. Who knew what would happen?

Decompression. I had a cold the last three weeks of shooting that I finally got rid of. Everybody left, of course, except John Hardy and I (and the Baton Rouge-based crew members). Things are quiet. The videocassettes of the remaining dailies won't be here until next week. The video set-up I'll be using is a two-machine ¾" non-time code system at Video Park, Inc., my alma mater. Park Seward, my former boss, gave us a great flat-rate deal, the sole proviso being that we use the room during off-hours. I spent most of the week making Betacam protection copies of what dailies I had and trying to log the film in some coherent fashion (Davis Guggenheim at Outlaw is doing the computerized version, which I am due to receive shortly).

It's very quiet. I was sad to see everyone go (although, being my usual self, nobody could tell). I think many of the cast and crew, in spite of the fact that they had a good time, aren't sure how the film will come out. I think they're *hoping* it'll be good. So am I. So is Larry Estes.

Saw *Married to the Mob* again, and liked it much better this time. I've borrowed David Foil's copy of *Swimming to Cambodia* to watch in the editing room whenever I need inspiration or just a plain old break from *sex, lies.*

I went to New York for two days to see friends and get a brief change of venue. I saw *The Last Temptation of Christ* at the Ziegfeld, and *loved* it. Great film. Very uplifting, I thought. There were people

205

picketing outside the theater, and I just don't understand how anyone with half a brain (or more) couldn't get something positive out of that film. It was the first time I felt I could relate to Christ, that he wasn't unreachable or unknowable (perhaps that is what some people object to). Well, I was very moved by it, and fuck what anybody else thinks. One interesting note: The Ziegfeld Theatre, the premier movie house in New York, has one incredibly bad projection lens. On every odd changeover reel, you'd get this shitty lens that would project about one-third of the image completely out of focus. You could tell the guy was trying to adjust it, because when the projectionist would try to focus, the blurry section would just move from left to right. Unbelievable and very irritating.

12–18 SEP 88

We got the rest of the dailies. If the scene between Ann and Graham on the couch ends up working, it will largely be due to Walt Lloyd. He really hit one out of deep left-center. I feel like he peaked right when the film itself is supposed to peak. Boy, did I get lucky.

I finished logging and making protection copies of all the dailies. I've avoided starting until Monday. I've told everyone that I'll have a first cut in four weeks, and I think that was a mistake.

A strange thing happened. I got a call from Larry Estes. He said he had looked at the dailies, and was I *sure* he had gotten all the footage, because he didn't see any nudity. I said that was because there wasn't any. He said well, why was that? I said, well, I made the decision that it wasn't necessary or appropriate, and shot the film accordingly, and felt like it would still be erotic, just not explicit. He said I had a commitment to shoot what was written. I said I felt the script was purposefully vague as far as the sexual scenes were concerned, and that, for instance, the word "breast" didn't appear in the script. Well, he said, we might have a problem, and I'll be very interested to see the rough cut. That, essentially, was the conversation. Bob Newmyer immediately called to say that he was sorry the conversation had taken place, that as a producer it was his job to make sure that I didn't have to have conversations like that, and that it wouldn't happen again. He said not to worry.

Now, this situation is not as cut-and-dried as it may seem. When Larry Estes was bugging his boss every day for two months trying to get this movie made, one of the selling points was that in a worst-case scenario, RCA/Columbia could recoup their investment by pushing the sexual angle. So he was hoping, I think, for a certain amount of skin as an insurance policy, and at that point, I thought there probably *would* be some skin (I mean, hell, *The Last Picture Show* has nudity in it) so I wasn't discouraging him. The saleable elements of this film, especially if it doesn't receive a decent theatrical release (or any at all), are minimal. I didn't tell Larry that I agreed to give Laura a "no nudity" clause in her contract, so I kind of knew this was coming. I just hoped he would be *so happy* with the footage that he would forget it (pull out your Webster's dictionary, look up "naive," and stare at my picture). It was a difficult phone call because Larry Estes and I like and respect each other a great deal, we both want the film to be good, and each of us has, I think, a well-taken point. If he chose to take the film away (which he could do), I would simply remove my name and publicly disown it. I don't think it will come to that. What really upset me, I think, was the fact that the first phone call I got after shooting was not "Congratulations for coming in on time and on budget! The stuff looks great!" but rather, "What happened to the tits?" I did not want to be in this frame of mind at the beginning of editing.

19 SEP–16 OCT 88

Editing. One of the dangers of cutting your own movie is that you can't start until shooting has finished and everyone has gone home, and if you find yourself lacking footage and you're a low-budget film, well, you're just shit outta luck. So I had my fingers crossed.

One of the *good* things about editing your own movie is that editing, in my opinion, is where film really distinguishes itself as an art form. It's where the writing, acting, directing, photography, and sound are all brought together, and I think it's pretty damned exciting.

I started, of course, at the beginning. Right off the bat I had a problem that threatened to give me editor's block five minutes into my first day of editing (actually, it was more than five minutes in. I usually spend an inordinate amount of time "preparing" for the edit; needless organizing, etc. I'm always afraid to start. I'm the same way with writing, usually). The problem was where should I bring in Andie's voice? After a brief panic, I decided to just cut Jimmy's arrival and see where it seemed natural for her to come in. I cut the road P.O.V. shots together (I did six jump cuts here to get the best sections; five are invisible, and one is very visible: Where the camera starts to turn off the road and change surfaces I had to make a jump cut to eliminate a puddle that contained a reflection of the camera) and I stuck in a shot of Jimmy driving. I cut out of the P.O.V., went to the wide shot of Ray's, then into the shot of Jimmy taking the bag out of his trunk and entering the men's room. Suddenly all of the shots of him putting on his boots, pulling his keys from the ignition, etc., seemed irrelevant and wasteful. I must have been vamping or something. However, I was struck by the fact that the perfect place for Andie's voice to come in was where the P.O.V. shot came to a halt (and then began backing up). I knew I wanted to go to Andie clean after the men's room door shot, so I had to do a little nipping and tucking with the dialogue to come to there on "The last time I started feeling that way was . . ." The rest of this sequence went together pretty easily. I was suddenly happy that I had printed several takes of Andie's various angles, because I found different things in each that I liked, and I ended up building her stuff from a variety of sources.

From Peter's first appearance until the landlord sequence, things seemed to cut together very smoothly (I cut a few lines off the end of scene 8, and I can tell that matching audio on scene 10 will be a barrel of laughs because of weather weirdness on Jimmy's angle).

WHY DIDN'T I LISTEN TO ELIZABETH LAMBERT? The cafe scene (16) was a nightmare! Hand, arm, and wine-glass positions didn't match from one take to another, just like Elizabeth said and noted in her lined script. First, because I knew the scene was going to play long, I decided to come in on "Can I tell you something personal?" which eliminated 1¼ pages of script and about two minutes of screen time. The dumped material suddenly seemed very redundant. How come it didn't seem that way when we were shooting? Second, after testing various edits, it became apparent that due to continuity problems, I had to hold on angles for a while so that you quit looking for matching fuck-ups. Of the ten pauses that seemed to mean so much while we were shooting, six of them now seem interminable. There's a fine line between naturalistic dialogue and dialogue that is *so* realistic it puts you to sleep. I have to work on this. The edited cafe scene clocked in at six minutes. Fortunately, scenes 17–23 cut together smoothly. Scene 24 went together well, and I'm especially glad Jimmy asked for another take on the first section, because I ended up using it quite a bit. It was more different from the previous take than I had realized just watching it on the set. I'm finding that Jimmy, more than any of the other actors, really plays right to the lens. He's done some very subtle things with his eyes that I just didn't notice before. My only concern with scene 24 is that it runs almost nine minutes.

Scenes 25–31 cut together well. The first bar scene (32), as again predicted by Elizabeth Lambert, was a continuity nightmare. It took me eight hours to cut a three-minute sequence (I usually only cut about five hours a day. After that I get burned out and irritated that I'm not cutting on a more sophisticated system). The end result was fine, however.

Scene 34 became the first scene to be dumped. After watching Jimmy's reactions to Cynthia's tape in scene 27, there wasn't any point in even cutting it together. I knew that scene 34 didn't work. Had I been more confident, I probably wouldn't have even shot it. Scenes 35–44 went together as planned. I made a big cut in scene 45, that being Ann's monologue about her marriage being a blur, and vacuuming John's rug, etc. Suddenly that all seemed irrelevant, so I just went from Andie saying "John's a bastard" (which was added during shooting) to "Let's make a videotape." The rain on Andie's angle forced me to painstakingly steal every line of hers from other angles. Finding clean readings and then syncing them up took a long time, but eventually I got it to work.

There's a movie theater about two minutes from Video Park, which is good because I can duck out and catch a film whenever I feel like it. It's also bad because I can duck out and catch a film whenever I feel like it. I saw *Eight Men Out,* which I thought was John Sayles's best film to date, and I also saw *Dead Ringers,* which I thought was David Cronenberg's best film to date. I wonder what kind of theater *sex, lies* will play in if it hits Baton Rouge?

Scenes 46–55 didn't prove to be too difficult. I cut out a lot of pauses, but basically I covered myself pretty well.

Now, what music should I use for the scratch mix? For the opening I considered Leo Kottke, but I couldn't find anything that fit the mood exactly, so I ended up using a small section of an orchestral piece by John Adams called *Common Tones in Simple Time.* For the remainder of the scratch track, I pulled pieces from various Brian Eno albums, most particularly from his Ambient 1–4 series, and his Harold Budd collaborations. John Hardy and I sat in the editing room and watched the couch scene between Graham and Ann with music for the first time and actually smiled like idiots. John said "It works!"

I actually did it in four weeks. Not bad for a lazy, procrastinating first-timer. If I had worked harder (like *eight* hours a day), I probably could have done it in three weeks or less. Maybe next time.

17 OCT 88

I made six VHS hi-fi (mono) dubs. They went to:

> Nancy T.
> Outlaw
> Sound Dept. (Larry Blake, Mark Mangini)
> Morgan Mason
> Nick Wechsler
> Music Dept. (Cliff Martinez)

Larry Estes will look at Outlaw's copy.

I put a video crawl in front of the film. It read:

"This is a ROUGH EDIT, compiled from an untimed workprint and unmixed audio tracks. Although I have added some scratch music and sound effects, I cannot overemphasize the importance of properly composed and designed music and sound effects to the overall film. The rough edit is best viewed like any other theatrical feature; in a darkened room, without interruption or distraction."

The first cut is 115 minutes long.

18–26 OCT 88

Comments. The most enthusiastic responses came from Morgan Mason and the Outlaw contingency. Nick was very happy. Larry, Mark, Annette, Aaron, Alex, and Cliff all watched the film at Weddington and liked it, although they were cautious in their praise, I thought. Nancy T. liked it well enough, but complained about color and sound and I don't know how much of that is her taste and how much is her television. Larry Estes liked the film (as did his wife) and said nothing about nudity. Everybody agreed the film is too long.

Well, nobody *hated* it, at least. John Hardy and I sat down and began recutting almost immediately. First big change: I cut Graham's speech about time in scene 10 (unbearably pretentious monologue. Why didn't somebody stop me?). Second big change: The scene where Ann watches Graham sleep (no. 12) didn't work where it was. It was too early in the film for her to be that interested in him. John and I decided that the scene should go after scenes 16–17 (the cafe/Cynthia leaving John), since Ann is now intrigued after talking at length with Graham. It worked much better, and we wondered how we ever thought it should be anywhere else. I cut a full minute out of the cafe scene (all the stuff where Graham tells Ann how beautiful she is, etc. We went right from Graham saying "I think you believe people are looking at you" to Ann's line "My therapist . . ." This deletion must have been planned by the gods, because the continuity matched perfectly). I cut all of scene 20, which broke my heart. Ron was incredible and the scene worked great, but it didn't propel the plot forward, and ultimately it made Ann look a little stupid. I cut scenes 29 and 30, because they broke the rhythm and feeling of the sex scene, which seemed to flow much more naturally into the Cynthia/Ann phone conversation (the camera movements between the two scenes were so identical it looked like I planned them to be cut back-to-back. Invisible hands, once again). Also, scenes 29/30 were just redundant after scene 19. It was clear how Ann felt about Cynthia's sexuality. Why weren't these redundancies clearer in script form? It may be because the actors bring so much that is unspoken that you just can't tell what's redundant until you string it end to end. In the future, though, I'm definitely going to keep this problem in my mind while writing.

The remainder of the film stayed pretty much the same, save for some shortening of pauses and stuff.

I had a talk with Cliff Martinez. He said he was surprised at the choice of scratch music. When Cliff and I originally talked, I was thinking of a score along the lines of Stewart Copeland's *Rumble Fish*. But when I cut the film together, I saw that really wasn't appropriate, that the film needed something evocative but unobtrusive. Cliff said he will start cranking.

After the re-edit, I logged the film (by hand. This was not fun. Each edit requires approximately forty characters of information, and there were over forty pages containing fifteen edits apiece) and made dubs of the second edit. I don't see that there is any more left to cut out. The current version is 108 minutes, without any sort of credits, obviously. I wonder if Larry Estes will hold me to the letter of the law if I'm not under 105 minutes?

Mark has separated from Annette, so he and I will be sharing a place in Studio City while I finish the film. This is one of those situations where an unfortunate development for someone else turns out to be great for you. I really couldn't ask Larry to let me stay on his couch again, even though we'll be spending every day (and most nights) together for the next however many months.

Nancy T. is trying to get us into the United States Film Festival, which takes place in January in Park City, Utah (where Park Seward, my former boss, vacations every year. Coincidence?). A friend of hers,

Marjorie Skouras (whom I've met), is on the board, and has expressed an interest in seeing the film. It looks like we'll have to give them a cassette, which is a bummer, but I doubt we could be ready in time anyway, and I heard they've pretty much chosen all the films for competition.

27 OCT–1 NOV 88 NEW YORK

Came to New York en route to Los Angeles to see some friends and prepare for the long haul. I don't think I'll be going back to Baton Rouge again to live.

I sent out the second version, and I'll get comments when I hit Los Angeles, I'm sure.

Interesting note: Bumped into the composer John Adams in the elevator of the hotel where I was staying. I told him that I had flown from Baton Rouge to Houston to see *Nixon in China* and had loved it (which was true). He seemed very nice, and genuinely surprised that someone had recognized him. I think he is ripe to do a great film score. Maybe I can get him to do one for me someday.

2–6 NOV 88 LOS ANGELES

Consensus is that the film is still too long, and more importantly, I have come to the decision that the earring discovery scene does not work. Andie gave me exactly what I asked for, I just asked for the wrong thing. She will be in Los Angeles next week shooting a commercial for a new perfume that she'll be promoting, so we'll try and do it then.

The deadline for submitting films to the U.S. Film Festival was Nov. 1st. We did submit it in time, but we won't know if the film has been accepted until next week. Apparently there are six films vying for the last open spot. Marjorie liked the film very much, which was nice to hear. I had met Marjorie a few years ago when J. Paul Higgins and I were trying to get financing for *Putting on Airs* (aka *Druthers;* aka *Inside Out.* I never could decide what to call the damn thing, and I never really got the script to work either, though that didn't prevent me from trying to get it made. I eventually threw it away). Marjorie liked the script, and we liked Marjorie, but their company was really only buying finished films. She gave us a very positive letter to show to investors as evidence of her interest, which I thought was nice. Again, it's strange how things come around.

The Cinerama Dome was holding a retrospective of films that had premiered there, so Larry, Mark, and I went to see *Jaws,* which Mark had *never* seen. There was a big crowd, and it was wonderful seeing it again. That was my 28th time seeing that film in a theater (*Apocalypse Now* is second, with 17 theatrical viewings). I've been in situations where people asked me what I did for a living, and when I told them, they would ask "What's your favorite film?" More often than not I would say *Jaws,* which never failed to surprise. Usually people expect *Grand Illusion* or something like that. A *serious* film, in other words.

7–10 NOV 88

I spoke to Andie, and we will shoot the inserts for scene 42 on the 11th at the apartment where Mark and I are living (amazingly, the carpeting is the same color as Sonny's master bedroom carpeting).

Nick, Morgan, and I had lunch with Marjorie Skouras. She said she wasn't allowed to tell us anything about the festival, but I came away feeling things looked pretty good.

I rented some off-line edit time to try and make some further trims. Davis Guggenheim and I sat for a couple of hours and did some nipping and tucking. The film is now down to 105 minutes. I talked to Steve New about the edit list, and I'll have to copy the whole thing over again. In order for him to accurately read my list, I have to separate the last two digits of every ingoing and outgoing edit, because those are the actual frame numbers (as opposed to foot numbers). My hand hurts just thinking about it.

I called and rented all the camera and lighting gear for the inserts, so we're all set. Larry will sit in as guest production mixer. I've decided I'll just cut this new stuff directly into the conformed workprint when it comes back from Steve New, and skip the transfer to video.

11 NOV 88

Today we shot the inserts. Andie did a remarkable job, and it was wonderful seeing her again. She was quite pregnant, so we had to shoot from the shoulders up (which is what I was planning anyway). I had bought a green backdrop, and I still had the clothes that she wore for the scene previously, so it was a good cheat, I thought. Walt and I referred to a videocassette of the original footage to check continuity and lighting, and it looked perfect to me. How Andie was able to come up with the reactions she did in such cramped, hot quarters with six people three feet away, I'll never know. We ended up shooting three shots, essentially: Andie's face, a tight shot of the earring being smashed, and an over-the-shoulder of her pulling the earring out of the vacuum cleaner teeth.

After returning from lunch, I got a call saying that we got into the U.S. Film Festival. Holy shit!! I'm really psyched, but Larry and I will have to kill ourselves to be ready in time (and I think a temp mix will have to suffice). I spoke to Larry Estes, and he agrees with me that we should hold off on changing the title, at least until after the festival. It wasn't Larry Estes that thought the title should be changed, actually. The marketing folks at RCA/Columbia *thought* that the vendors would *say* that the buying public would *think* that the film was shot on videotape. That's *triple*-guessing, by my estimation. They suggested changing the *last word* in the title. They said they liked the first two words fine, they could sell those. The mind boggles. Anyway, Larry Estes is going to run interference for me.

12–15 NOV 88

I finished the recopied edit logs and dropped them off. We got the insert footage back from CFI and the stuff looks great. I finally let Pat Dollard look at the film, which is only fair, seeing as how he's my agent. He liked the film, saying that he was especially impressed with the performances, which was exactly what I wanted to hear. He asked what I wanted to do next. I hadn't thought about that.

16–20 NOV 88

The calm before the storm. All we can do is wait for the conformed workprint to come back. I've asked Mark to write an acoustic piece for the opening of the film. He's a wicked guitar player, and a while back he played the beginnings of a very interesting piece for me on his twelve-string. Our friendship has enabled me to set up a very favorable arrangement with Weddington, which Mark owns one-third of. Basically, he's giving Larry and me the studio time for $25,000 in exchange for two points of profit participation (4% of the creative cut). This money insures that Weddington will make no out-of-pocket expenditures for supplies, but with studio time going at upwards of $175 an hour, it's still a gamble. Part of the reason he's giving us the deal is to definitively test the new multi-track editing system they recently installed. It is Larry's desire to cut every sound in this movie on multi-track instead of mag, including dialogue. After some discussion, we decided that the foley should probably be cut on mag, but *everything* else will be cut on multi-track. Larry is a tad concerned, only because there is no reference for how long this will take. Since dialogue isn't normally cut like this, we're not sure how to estimate the time needed. At any rate, this "experiment" is part of the reason Mark is giving us the deal. I sure hope those points end up meaning something.

The funny thing is, it still doesn't feel like a real movie. It feels like an elongated short film. We had a small crew shooting mostly indoors with a small cast, no money to spare, and here in postproduction it's just Larry and I. The two of us will have to do *everything*. I think it's good that it feels that way. There's less pressure.

I met with Tony Safford, the head of the U.S. Film Festival. We sat on the steps outside his office and had a nice, informal chat. He told me that things were going to be different for me after this film shows in Park City, that I should be careful not to get sucked into the jaws of Hollywood too much. I think he's overestimating the response, frankly, but I thought it was nice of him to offer the advice.

21 NOV–2 DEC 88

Got the workprint back, and all of the numbers seemed to work (well, *almost* all. In scene 41, every time we were supposed to be seeing Laura there was a shot of Jimmy shaving at the gas station. Some glitch in the numbers, I guess. I dug up Laura's angle and stuck in the appropriate shots). Next we transferred the ¾" rough-edit audio to 35mm mag to sync it up with the workprint. This took a while, since there are slight sync variances due to the number interpolation involved in getting 24 (film frames) into 30 (video frames) and back to 24 (film frames) again. In other words, you get an extra frame on the end of an edit occasionally. Larry and I got Mark "Mr. Sync" Mangini to "frame-fuck" the whole film, which took a while because Mark *does* have a day job, one that requires a lot of attention. He did it, though, and Larry and I set the date for video transfer (the multi-track runs interlocked with ¾" video. So you see, the 24/30 issue never really goes away). I made some more cuts, primarily in the Ann/Graham section of scene 51, to bring the running time down to 104 minutes. I cut in the new footage of Andie for scene 42 and everyone (meaning

Mark, Larry, and I) agreed that the new material was a vast improvement. However, just the brief experience of sticking in those few shots reminded me of how much I hate cutting on film. I prefer even the most basic video editing system, and hopefully in the future I'll get to use the Montage, which is a nonlinear video editing system.

Saw *The Naked Gun*, which was hysterical. Unfortunately, I would be accused of ripping it off if I were to make *Dead From The Neck Up* now, and I told Bob this. He was bummed, but understood completely.

3 DEC 88

A dark, dark day. The Blimp (Larry's '73 Bel Air) died. The car, to put it mildly, had a history. It had been terminally ill and the object of much derision for some time, so its demise was not really a surprise. For my money, the car's high point came in February '87, when Larry and I drove it to the Grammys (I had been nominated for the concert film that I'd made for Yes that Larry had worked on as well), and the crowd outside the Shrine auditorium cheered us loudly (the car had a lot of visible body damage and was prone to belching blue smoke). Frankly, I'm a bit relieved, because I've been trying to force Larry to get a different car. He called Mark and me from a phone booth at Laurel and Moorpark, and we went down and helped him push it out of the street, a large pool of black blood marking its death spot. Looks like we'll be using public transit for a while. I'm planning to get a used car, but I have to wait until I find out how much I owe for last year's taxes (I filed late, so I'm expecting big penalty charges).

Further editing has brought the length down to 103 minutes.

6-11 DEC 88

We transferred the workprint to video at Telecine Tech. I'm really worried that we won't be ready for Park City in time, and although Larry assures me we will, I think he's got *his* fingers crossed as well. I forced him to do some test edits against his will, and we're both satisfied that the system will work.

12-14 DEC 88

Sound editing officially started on the 12th with the therapy scene. This is truly tedious work, finding every line on ¼" audio, then syncing it with the work track, but somebody's got to do it.

I discussed with Mark the potential cost of having Johnny Dunn cut one of the reels (probably 4AB) on mag. I'd prefer to not spend the money, but it realistically doesn't look like Larry can cut the entire show in under four weeks, and I think it's worth the money to have a little breathing room.

15 DEC 88

Strange day. It started off with gum surgery, which I highly recommend. Then I was sitting in a yogurt shop gingerly spooning yogurt into my mouth when I spotted this guy about to walk into the place, and I caught his eye for a moment and thought "I hope he puts that cigarette out before entering." Well, he came in, and after doing something for a few minutes (I was semi-turned away from him), he walked by my table and casually as you please, picked up my address book from the table and began walking out with it. I grabbed his arm and shouted at him, and he then sprinted out the door and into the parking lot. I started after him, shouting (my mouth started to bleed at this point). He ran for the alley that runs parallel to Ventura Blvd., and he just had too much of a jump on me. I yelled "I got a good look at you, motherfucker!!" and he gave me the finger and started walking away. Livid beyond reason, I ran back to the parking lot and jumped in Mark's Cabriolet, which I was borrowing for the day. I turned onto Ventura, headed in the direction the guy was walking. I turned left twice and headed back up the alley, hoping to run into him (literally, perhaps?). I slowed to a crawl and looked around carefully. Suddenly I thought I saw him between two buildings, so I made a U-turn, and as I started to accelerate, he stepped out in front of the car and looked up. I pointed at him through the windshield and said *"You,* mother-fucker!" (I was big on the MF word, for some reason.) He looked at me, reached into his jacket, and started walking around to the driver's side, and I'm thinking that I won't make the screening for Mike Watts tonight. The guy pulls out my address book. I look at him and say "There's nothing in it." He hands it to me and says "It's all there." The look on his face was strange, like Why did I do this? I said Thank you, and he said You're welcome, and I drove off. It took about an hour for my adrenaline rush to wear off. It was at that point that my mouth started to hurt.

We screened the film for Mike Watts, which would have been

plenty enough excitement for one day, believe me. He actually liked the film, said he felt there were some cuts to be made, but thought the performances were excellent. The biggest topic of discussion was whether or not to cut the Cynthia taping scene in half, ending it where she says "I prefer to sit" and walking camera left. I'm willing to make the cut (I suggested it, in fact), as long as the audience won't feel cheated. Larry feels like Cynthia on the couch talking about her sexual experiences is one of the more powerful and erotic scenes in the film, and thinks it's a bad idea. Bob and Morgan could go either way. Mike Watts wants to know if it will be difficult to get a couple of prints for the American Film Market (AFM) in February, and I said it isn't, although I told him that I anticipate making cuts after Park City, and he may have to screen an "old" version. He said fine. I think things went very well.

16–24 DEC 88

Slugging it out, seven days a week. Long hours of me feeding Larry the numbers and him making the edits. In addition to my mouth ailment, I came down with an embarrassing malady that is commonly treated with a product ending with a capital H. Often I was lying on my back in front of the mixing console in an attempt to limit various sorts of bleeding. It's a glamorous life, this directing stuff.

In my spare time I worked on some temp titles. Virgin had done a really neat graphic treatment of the title with this kind of distressed typewriter font, and I'm attempting to duplicate that by typing out the various title cards on a piece of paper and then blowing them up seven or eight times on the Xerox machine. It looks okay, but I don't know how legible they will be.

I decided to get Johnny Dunn to cut reel 4AB. Larry sort of objected at first, but then realized we really didn't have any choice. Larry normally makes a pilgrimage to his hometown of New Orleans every Christmas, but he has chosen not to do so this year, for fear of losing his job and his closest friend. No, really, he knew a while back that he wouldn't be able to go; I just feel bad that he can't.

Larry has rented a car from Ugly Duckling. He's using his busy schedule as an excuse not to look into getting a used car, but that's understandable at this point, since time is tight. I myself must begin looking for a vehicle (my taxes weren't as severe as I thought they would be).

25 DEC 88

Larry and I worked, stopping only to have Christmas dinner at the Copper Penny across from the Burbank Studios. The turkey wasn't bad, actually.

26 DEC–8 JAN 89

Getting there.

I bought a 1960 AMC Rambler. Aaron and Ezra both took a look at it and said I scored big. I took that as a good sign, since they both know how to dismantle and reassemble entire automobiles. It runs beautifully; it just needs a paint job.

I turned the titles over to CFI, and they made reversal transparencies and shot them, and I cut them onto the workprint. I then turned the workprint over to Steve New and Scott Hill, and they started conforming the negative. Shit's gettin' serious.

Larry is cutting fast and furious. We bought this digital sampler that Akai makes, and it is making life a lot easier. Larry can take a half-second's worth of silence between words, then cut it and loop it so that it can last for however long he needs it to. Spiffy.

Larry Estes inquired as to whether it was a good idea to show the film to Orion Classics before Park City. I said I thought it was better to premiere it at the festival without anyone having seen it, in the hopes that if it went over well, a bidding war would start. I also told him that I would probably be hand-carrying a wet print to the festival anyway, so Orion Classics couldn't really see it beforehand even if we wanted them to. Everyone else seemed to feel the same *vis-à-vis* the bidding-war scenario, so Larry Estes said fine, let's wait. I don't know if there will *be* any bidding war, but it sure sounded good.

A new and improved Ten Favorites as of 1 JAN 89:

All the President's Men
Annie Hall
Citizen Kane
The Conversation
The 5,000 Fingers of Dr. T
The Godfather (parts I & II)
Jaws
The Last Picture Show

Sunset Boulevard
The Third Man

So *A Thousand Clowns* and *A Hard Day's Night* drop to make room for *The Conversation* and *The Last Picture Show*. That's show biz.

9–15 JAN 89

The insanity has begun. Walt and I met at CFI to start timing the picture. I requested that Dan Muscarella be our timer, since he timed *The Moderns*. Dan was quite ill, but the workprint was very close to how Walt wanted the picture to look, so it shouldn't be too big a job.

Larry has pulled several all-nighters, and I have done my share by cutting all the effects. At one point, Larry objected to some hammering sounds that I had laid over the scenes at Cynthia's apartment. I told him that I wanted those particular sounds over those particular scenes, because I felt Cynthia lived in a neighborhood where construction was going on. He shrugged.

Jimmy and Peter came in to loop a grand total of about eight lines each. They both seemed to like the brief scenes that they saw. Jimmy thought Peter's "family crisis" line was hysterical.

I'm excited about the festival. Larry, Mark, Walt, and Cliff are going to go, as well as Peter and Laura. I've been leafing through the program, staring at the page where *sex, lies* appears in the Dramatic Competition section. Marjorie Skouras wrote a great synopsis for the film. I can't believe we're actually going.

16–20 JAN 89

More insanity. Larry stayed up for days at one point, finishing the dialogue pre-dubs. For some reason Johnny Dunn's reel sounded strange, not editorially, but like some of the transfers had been Dolby-encoded and others not. We had no choice but to go with it, though. At one point we were supposed to do the final temp dub, and these two union guys from the sound mixers local came into the room and "busted" the shop, saying that we couldn't edit on a mixing console without a mixer, and that Larry had to join the union, etc. It was all very *Brazil*-like and Larry and I were so toasted by then that the delay was actually a godsend, since it forced us to finish the following day, when our ears were a little more fresh. We rushed the mag over to

Warner Hollywood and shot the optical, which was then ready to be married to . . .

. . . the print. More nightmares. The first print Walt and I looked at was so horrendous we practically drew straws to see who would take the gas pipe first. It turned out that Dan Muscarella was so ill that another timer was forced to take over, and he really wasn't familiar with what we were trying to do. Walt and I insisted that a new print be struck and gave detailed instructions as to how it should be altered (hell, if it had just looked like the workprint we'd have been happy). The second print came back the next day, and it was better, but still not good enough. By this time Dan was back on the job, and we ordered another print for pick-up on Saturday morning, and hoped that everything would work out.

21 JAN 89 PARK CITY

Got up this morning, picked up the print at CFI, and met Walt at Warner Hollywood to screen the movie at 7:30. The print looked okay, so I took it on the plane with me to Park City.

Todd Elvins, a festival volunteer, picked me up at the airport. We talked a while (he has heard that tickets for *sex, lies* were selling well), and when we got in and dropped my bags off, I followed him to the hospitality room to hang out and drink beer with the rest of the volunteers. I ended up just telling all the people I met that I was a volunteer driver, mostly because I didn't feel like talking about the film. I even had my picture taken with the volunteers.

The festival will put the filmmaker up for five days, so for the first half of the festival I've rented a place on my own. As it turned out, the place is huge, and I feel a bit stupid staying here by myself. It's peaceful, though.

22 JAN 89

First public showing of *sex, lies.* I got up beforehand to introduce the film and explained that the sound mix was temporary, and that I was going to re-do the titles, but that everything else was fair game. The audience seemed to like it. There were good laughs (in some unexpected places; I never thought of Graham's "key" speech as being very funny, but apparently it is), and applause at the end. I answered some questions afterward, and when I was done people came up to me and said they liked the film, which was nice. Some guy named Sam Kitt from Universal introduced himself and said he wanted to talk with me later. I think I was more curious than nervous about the response. I mean, the film is what it is, I can't really change it, so it's really out of my hands in that regard.

When I got back to my room, the door was wide open ("Unknown Filmmaker Surprises Burglar; Shits Himself"). After turning on lights and making lots of noise (to give the possible intruder plenty of warning, so he could escape without my ever seeing him), I found that the place was empty. I must not have shut the door very tightly.

23 JAN 89

I got up and called everyone to let them know that the film seemed to go over okay. I saw a few films and generally kind of goofed off all day. The festival people who saw the film said they enjoyed it, and I'm now trying to talk them into actually letting me do some volunteer driving, since I had my picture taken with the other volunteers.

I met with these two guys, Ron Yerxa and Albert Berger, who would like me to read a book they're in the process of optioning called *This Boy's Life*, by Tobias Wolff. I've read some of Wolff's short stories and I think he's a great writer, so I'm interested in looking at this novel. I had a good feeling about these guys. They seemed very down-to-earth.

Two people stopped me on the street to tell me they liked the film. I heard Friday's showing has sold out.

Every night there is a festival party of some sort provided by a sponsor. I usually hang out with the volunteers, since they are the only people I know in Park City. So far, when I am introduced as the maker of *sex, lies*, people usually say "I've heard good things about your film." That's a nice feeling.

24 JAN 89

Saw *A Woman Under the Influence*, which completely blew me away. I had to walk around for a while after it was over. I don't know how to describe Gena Rowlands's performance. Truly incredible.

I convinced one of the coordinators of the festival to let me do some volunteer driving. I took some of the Latin American contingent to their lodging, did a ticket run (what a power trip. I could've brought the entire festival to a halt), and drove Jodie Foster and Beth Henley to a screening (they were both very nice). During my ticket run I ran into Peter and his wife, Paula Harwood, who had just arrived in town and were obviously surprised to see me running around doing volunteer work. I would've talked to them longer, but I had a job to do!

25 JAN 89

Had my first interview (accompanied by Peter), with Edward Guthmann of the *San Francisco Chronicle.* I think I was too serious.

Larry, Mark, Cliff, Bob, John Hardy, Nancy T., Nancy McIntosh, Steve Brill, Laura, and Davis all arrived today to see *sex, lies.* There was a huge crowd in the lobby, and the show sold out about thirty minutes before the screening started (Saturday's show has sold out as well, meaning three out of four screenings have sold out). The producers and I were a little nervous because the people from Orion Classics were there (well, for a little while, anyway. They got up and left twenty minutes into the film. I'm assuming the worst). Larry, Mark, Cliff, and Bob all came out saying the film worked better for them tonight than ever before. Mark said he was really caught up in it. After the screening I asked for a show of hands about the title. About one-third of the audience thought we should change it, as opposed to Sunday's screening, where a full one-half thought the title should be changed.

We all had dinner afterward and drank. Two more screenings and it's all over. I'm worried that the good word of mouth we've gotten so far will backfire on one of the upcoming screenings.

Larry, Mark, Cliff, and I are sharing bunk beds in a condo provided by the festival. Our other roommates are Tony Buba (here with *Lightning Over Braddock*), Ron Mann (here with *Comic Book Confidential*), and Christine Choy (here with *Who Killed Vincent Chin?*). I've heard that all of their films are very good. It's like camp, almost.

The first words from Nancy T.'s mouth after the screening: "Is there any way to get rid of the hammering in those scenes at Cynthia's?" I'll wait for a while before I tell Larry this.

26 JAN 89

I find that I need very little sleep these days, I'm so wired from what's going on. I've been going to bed late and popping up early to take a shower and go down to Main Street and have breakfast.

Today I had an interview with Aljean Harmetz of *The New York*

Times, which was interesting. Again, I felt like I was too serious. I have to work on this.

I'm starting to be approached by people in the film business about future work, which is really weird. I haven't really thought about that too much. I do think, based upon the response so far, that I will be able to get another film, I'm just not that excited about my other scripts right now. *Dead From The Neck Up,* as I said, is on the shelf, *State of Mind* and *Crosstalk* both need a lot of work, *Proof Positive* is a remake, so that would involve obtaining rights, etc., which could be expensive (and I haven't read it in three years. I'm not sure it's even any good). I'm pretty sure that I want to write the films I make, so I'm not really that keen on reading scripts. I've read four screenplays in the last four years that I thought were outstanding: *The Fabulous Baker Boys* by Steve Kloves, *Raising Arizona* by Joel & Ethan Coen (which I read while they were in production), *Kafka* by Lem Dobbs (amazing script. Nobody will ever make it), and *One Saliva Bubble* by David Lynch and Mark Frost (I think this was actually in preproduction at one point. Incredibly funny script). Now I'm sure that there are other great scripts out there, but in general, most scripts are pretty limp. The really good ones, ironically, tend to be dismissed as not being commercial enough.

27 JAN 89

Tonight's screening was lunacy. We were showing at a different theater with a smaller lobby, so the crunch was even worse than Wednesday. Paul Mazursky was there, which was frightening (I hadn't even considered that other filmmakers would see *sex, lies.* Is there any way to prevent this?). Larry and I found out that, believe it or not, the projector runs slow in this theater, meaning this dialogue-laden talku-drama played at an even more deliberate pace than intended. I kept sticking my head in and out while guarding the door (there were already people seated in the aisles. One lady kept wanting to "take a look," and when I kept refusing, she called me a prick). The audience seemed to like it, but again, it's hard to tell. See, festival audiences (here I'm talking like I've actually been to a festival before), or rather, *this* festival audience, is very sympathetic. I've seen films that weren't going down too well where the audience was really trying to hang in there. So I don't know how much is the film and how much is the audience being kind. Morgan was there for tonight's screening and he said it was going over great, no excuses needed. I hope he was right. I wonder what Mazursky thought?

At tonight's party I was introduced to Todd McCarthy, who writes for *Variety*. He said he liked *sex, lies,* and that his review would be favorable. He's not allowed to lie to my face, right? One more screening and it will all be over.

28 JAN 89

Today's screening was more insane than ever. I heard a rumor that people were scalping tickets to get in (which I doubt). Afterward I was surrounded in the street by people who wanted to tell me how much they liked the film, which was a nice but disorienting experience. It's not that I tire of people saying they like the film, it's just that in some ways the film is separate from me, and so sometimes I feel as though I am accepting praise that doesn't entirely belong to me. Pat Dollard was close by to make sure I didn't say anything stupid.

In the last few days people have been saying "You're gonna win!," which is something I didn't want to hear. At the awards ceremony we all sat together, and frankly, I was nervous as hell. Paul Mazursky was Master of Ceremonies, and he was pretty hysterical. I'm actually a little fuzzy on what happened. I know that *For All Mankind* won the two documentary awards, and then I think Mazursky announced the Dramatic Competition Audience Award by saying "I've seen it, and I loved it. *sex, lies, and videotape!*" At this point I stood and began to make my way to the podium. My ears felt hot, which means they were probably bright red. I accepted the award and said a few words, remembering to thank Marjorie Skouras for getting us into the festival. Then I sat down, and then *True Love* won the Grand Prize. Everybody was really happy. So far we've been approached by almost all the independent distributors and one major.

Randa Haines introduced herself and said she really liked the film, which made me feel really good.

The *sex, lies* crew stayed up very late and drank too much (except for Larry and I, who drank very little).

It's all over. Now I can relax.

29 JAN 89

My last day in Park City. My experience here has been incredible, to say the least. I have a very different idea of what will happen to me and to the film. I think some re-cutting is in order, and I'm glad that Larry can now really get started on the sound mix proper. I couldn't have fantasized this kind of response. I'll take some intense feelings and memories away with me (standing in the sunlight-streaked lobby before yesterday's screening, Dustin Hoffman's face on the omnipresent free issues of *Premiere*).

For the record, my favorite of the films I saw here was *Apartment Zero*.

30 JAN 89 LOS ANGELES

Boy, Todd McCarthy wasn't kidding. Larry showed up this morning with five copies of today's *Variety*, and well, he liked the film a lot. All I could do was read it and go "Holy shit . . . holy shit." Pat Dollard called not too long afterward to say that Sydney Pollack had phoned to see if he could screen a print. Pat also said that the calls were starting to come in from all over the place; people either wanting to see the film or talk to me. My initial reaction was to say that nobody sees the film until I've re-cut and the mix is finished. That may not be realistic, but since we only have the one print, it looks like for the time being there will only be distributor screenings.

31 JAN–5 FEB 89

Interesting week. I got a call from the development person from Wildwood, Robert Redford's company, and I'll meet with her next week. She, as it turned out, knows Ron Yerxa and Albert Berger, whom I'm also meeting with next week (I read *This Boy's Life* and loved it. I just don't see a way to make it into a film while retaining what is great about the book).

I was in a bookstore this week and while I was looking through the fiction section I spotted a paperback of *The Last Ship*. Of course! Whatever happened to that? I grabbed two copies (and paid for them) and immediately called Bob. I asked him if he and John Kao had had any success in trying to set up *The Last Ship* anywhere. He said as a matter of fact, they were days away from signing with a producer who wanted to make it into a miniseries. I asked Bob if he and John Kao could give me four weeks to try and set up *The Last Ship* as a feature with me to write and direct, with the understanding that I needed to get a "name" producer involved. I told him my dream scenario: Somebody like, for instance, Sydney Pollack, sees *sex, lies* (he hasn't yet), likes it, and likes *The Last Ship* enough to come on board (no pun intended). Now, I explained, I didn't think it will be Pollack (he's too big. I just can't imagine him wanting to get involved), but assuming it were someone *like* him, could they hold off? Bob said he'd talk to John Kao, but that his feeling was they would love to pursue it. Good. I'd been toying with some ideas for transforming *Crosstalk* into a different script, but *The Last Ship* excites me more.

Since RCA/Columbia Home Video is a subsidiary of Columbia Pictures, we were obviously obligated to show them the film. Well, as it turned out, they liked it. Too much, in fact. Let me explain. It is our desire that an independent distributor release the film. While we are very flattered by Columbia's interest, we know they really don't know how to release a "specialty" film (Larry Estes told me long ago never to say "art house" again). This was evidenced by the fact that they wished to have a test screening wherein they would pull people off the street and see how the film played. To say I was distressed by this idea is to put it mildly. I was told this was a *fait accompli*, that Columbia could do whatever they wanted, and that Larry Estes, the No. 2 man in Home Video, could not call up Dawn Steel and tell her not to screen the film. I called Larry Estes and laid twenty solid minutes on him about why I thought it was a bad idea for Columbia to do this screening. At the end he said that it would be very difficult for him to stop it, but that he would try. And bless his goddam heart, he got it stopped. Columbia shortly thereafter graciously agreed to let us take the distribution deal of our choice, and I got a very nice call from Dawn Steel, in which she said she liked the film very much and hoped there was something I could make with Columbia (I met with Amy Pascal at Columbia to discuss just such a possibility). Larry Estes is gaining on Walt as my personal hero.

I also met with Barbara Maltby of Wildwood. She had seen the film at Park City and liked it very much and wanted to know if there was anything their company could get involved with. I said that there was a novel called *King of the Hill* by A. E. Hotchner that I thought was great film material (Lisa Drew, a friend of mine, had given it to me to read in 1986). She hadn't heard of it, but said she would track it down and read it. I think it'll be right up their alley, actually. It's funny—it just popped into my head when she asked me. I'd loved the book, but had forgotten about it until that moment.

Met with Ron Yerxa and Albert Berger and told them my feelings about a film version of *This Boy's Life*. They understood how I felt. I told them that I had spoken with Barbara Maltby about *King of the*

Hill, and that perhaps they should read it as well. They said they would.

I called in my first perk. Columbia was holding a benefit screening of *Lawrence of Arabia* at the Century Plaza with Sir Dave expected to make an appearance, so I called up Amy Pascal and begged for two tickets. She came through and Larry and I went in our best suits and sat amongst famous people (Rob Lowe was right in front of us). I told Larry I felt a little guilty about calling in a favor, but he said as long as it was a movie like this, and not a girl or something, I would be absolved (in his book). That made me feel better. Sir Dave spoke before the screening and said he wished people would stop making films with so much sex in them. Larry and I decided not to invite him to our premiere.

We struck a second print for distributors' screenings in New York. We're still hoping Orion Classics will be interested (they left the screening in Park City because of an emergency).

13 FEB–5 MAR 89

More gum surgery (the last of it, supposedly).

Had a meeting with Pat Dollard and the heads of Leading Artists, the agency that represents me. When I had spoken to them immediately after Park City, I'd said that I'd probably make a medium-sized film next (thinking *State of Mind* or the rewritten *Crosstalk*), which they thought was a good idea. Then *The Last Ship* brainstorm hit me, and well, I think Jim Berkus and Robert Stein wish I'd set my sights a little lower. They like the book, they just think it's huge (I think it's deceptively huge. A lot of the book is very internal, and I don't think the film would be unwieldy at all). They're not sure it can be successfully set up. I told them I didn't disagree, but that I loved the book, thought it would make a great film, and wanted to try setting it up. They said okay, and asked if they could still send me other scripts to look at. I said sure.

I had a meeting with Sam Kitt and Jim Jacks at Universal (actually, it was more than a meeting. They bought me lunch in the fancy section of the commissary and guess who I saw? Paul Mazursky). They expressed their regret that Universal wasn't really interested in distributing since RCA/Columbia owned the video rights, but said they were really keen on having me do something at Universal. They stressed that in the past year or so, Universal has been trying to broaden its horizon a little (*The Last Temptation of Christ* and the upcoming Spike Lee film being used as examples), and they hoped I had something I could bring over to them. I told them I hoped so, too, I just wasn't sure what exactly I was going to do next. I mentioned *The Last Ship*, and told them of my scouting for a "name" producer. At any rate, I liked them both, and I'll stay in touch even if nothing happens with me there.

Rolling Stone called a while back wanting to do a piece on me for the "Hot" issue. My first reaction was DON'T DO IT. Then I mulled it over for a while, and thought maybe it would be kind of neat, having my picture in *Rolling Stone* where people I went to school with would see it and stuff. So I said okay. Terri Minsky, the writer, spent the better part of a week here interviewing me. She liked the film, fortunately, and we got along great. She'd written a piece for *Spy* magazine that I actually referred to positively in a conversation, not knowing that she had written it. The only scary thing was that I thought it was just going to be a little story, and she said it was supposed to be like five thousand words. That's a lot.

I managed to weather the AFM, which I was dreading. See, here is where I thought the backlash would definitely occur. You've got an audience of buyers (in some cases non-English-speaking) from around the world who have to see dozens of films in a few days. By design, people watch films for a few minutes and leave. Well, it turned out that every screening was SRO, nobody walked out, and there was even some applause, which Nancy T. said was unheard of for an AFM screening. Part of the reason the screenings were packed was because a lot of nonbuyers, i.e., Hollywood folk, snuck in to see the film. This praise is getting out of hand. I mean, it's just this little film made by a few people that Larry and I are trying to finish. I don't know that it can stand up to great expectations. On the other hand, this is a good problem to have.

We closed the deal with Miramax. I think the deal we got was ruthless: one million advance, one million P&A (prints and ads) commitment, and an extremely favorable gross deal. Harvey Weinstein, who runs Miramax with his brother Bob, was in Los Angeles for the AFM, and he said he wouldn't go back to New York until he had the movie. For their trouble they get all rights for North America except home video. There are some (other independent distributors) who think Miramax went overboard. I guess we'll see. I don't know if it can make the kind of money they need to return their investment.

Sydney Pollack finally saw the film and liked it, apparently. I will meet with him on March 8th.

I've completed the post-Park City revisions. I cut off the beginning of the landlord scene a little, and made further trims in the Ann/Graham dialogue scene (Larry made some very good suggestions for a couple of crucial cuts). Locked picture! 100 minutes in length.

6–12 MAR 89

Met with Sydney Pollack. He was incredibly nice, and very complimentary about *sex, lies.* He asked me a few things about it, and I pumped him for stories and asked why he didn't shoot *Out of Africa* in the anamorphic format. The funny thing was, I think we both consider story, character, and performance to be the top priority in a film, and yet we're both very technically oriented as well. We spent a lot of time talking about the physical aspects of making a movie. He was very funny and tells a great story. He said he hoped there was something we could work together on, and I kind of choked. I mean, I didn't hit him with *The Last Ship* like I was planning to, so I left feeling kind of stupid. See, Sydney Pollack is the first person I've met that I thought "Wow. Sydney Pollack!" I mean, I've met a lot of important executives in the last several weeks, and that's great, but they change jobs so much, it's hard to get excited about someone who may not be there in a month. I can't think of anyone who the industry has more respect for. So I was a little nervous. So what I ended up doing was sending him a letter saying I had enjoyed our meeting, and telling him about *The Last Ship.* I enclosed a synopsis and some reviews of the book (and the book itself, although I know he's not going to sit and read a 616-page novel while he's trying to preproduce a $30 million movie with Robert Redford), and asked him to tell me what he thought of the project. Bob, John Kao, and I held our breath.

Meanwhile, Larry continues to mix like a fool. I feel bad that he's doing most of the work at this point while I run around "taking meetings" and "talking deals," but I guess I don't feel too bad about it, or I'd be in the mixing room twelve hours a day.

Got a call from Mark Johnson, who is Barry Levinson's producer. He saw the film recently and would like to meet with me. He sounded nice on the phone (a lot of people do, I'm finding). I'm also due to have lunch with Demi Moore. She called me herself at Weddington, which I gave her brownie points for. She sounded nice, also.

13–19 MAR 89

I met with Demi Moore and her development person, Bridget Adams.
They talked to me about a project they were trying to get into shape
and asked if I would read the script. The premise sounded intriguing
and I said sure. We had a tasty lunch (we were at The Ivy), and
eventually Pat Dollard joined us to say hello and meet Demi and
Bridget. On the way out I saw Morgan, who happened to be eating
there as well, and he teased me mercilessly about going Hollywood
(although not without irony. He knows that *he* is Mr. Hollywood. Or
is it Nick? I'm not sure).

I met with Mark Johnson and Stuart Cornfeld, who was a producer on *The Elephant Man* and *The Fly*. Stuart is part of the Levin-
son/Johnson team, which is looking to make some non-Barry-
directed movies. He hadn't seen *sex, lies* yet, which was frustrating for
him. Anyway, they asked me what I was doing next, and was it anything they could be involved with, and I said that, well, I really wanted
to make this book *The Last Ship* but that I had already approached
Sydney Pollack (we haven't heard from him yet, but until he responds
I can't really pursue any other options). They seemed intrigued and
asked if they could read the book anyway. I said sure. They asked if
there were anything else I was interested in and I said well, I'd read
this script a couple of years ago called *Kafka* that I thought was pretty
amazing, and Stuart said "Lem Dobbs is a friend of mine!" It turned
out Stuart has known Lem really well for years, so we started talking
about the script (this time Mark Johnson was in the dark, not having
read the script). I told them basically that I'd love to make that script
into a movie if they were interested. They said they were, and we
agreed to meet soon with Lem Dobbs present and after Stuart had
seen the movie and Mark had read the script and they both had read
the book.

Bonnie Schiffman took my picture for *Rolling Stone,* which was
not something I relished doing. She was great and made me as comfortable as possible; I just hate having my picture taken. We ended up
on Mulholland with my Rambler, and at one point some guy drove
by and yelled "You look like shit!" I love this town.

20–26 MAR 89

I talked to Larry Estes about giving me some money for a preview
trailer. I personally don't think the film synopsizes well visually, and

so I'd like to shoot some very graphic and striking conceptual footage of the inside of a video camera. He sounded intrigued and told me to draw up a budget.

David Gray of Dolby came by Weddington and installed the Dolby gear and lined up the room. Like the true *guys* that we are, Larry and I get a big kick out of all the fancy-looking equipment.

Larry is doing a bang-up job of mixing the film, and I'm doing a bang-up job of watching him. When we first started this thing back in December, I got into the terrible habit of walking up to the screen in the mixing room and breaking wind whenever I felt so compelled (the effects of this habit impacted more on Larry than myself). We wondered, at the time, if Ingmar Bergman was in the habit of passing gas on the dub stage, and if so, did the mix crew give him a hard time? So whenever my bad habit reappears, Larry and I start riffing imagined reprimands: "Ingmar!! Cut that out, you knucklehead!! That Bergman, he's a caution!" Working long hours under pressure will do this to you.

27 MAR–2 APR 89

Heard from Sydney Pollack. He is interested and wants to meet with Bob and me to discuss his potential involvement.

Also heard from Barbara Maltby (I was beginning to wonder what happened to her). She read *King of the Hill* and loved it, and is in the process of getting Redford to read it. I've told her what I know about Hotchner from Lisa Drew, which is that he has been approached before about this book, but never accepted any offers because he was afraid it would get sodomized (*King of the Hill* is quite autobiographical, apparently). Barbara is confident that Redford will like the book, and that his involvement will convince Hotchner that the adaptation will be of the highest quality (God knows *my* involvement doesn't guarantee it).

Walt and I went to CFI to start the timing process for the Interpositive and Internegative. Dan Muscarella is on the job, so we're hoping everything goes smoothly. It's a costly process, because to really check the Interpositive, you have to make the Internegative, and then make a print from that. We're due to see a check print next week.

Watched the Academy Awards with Annette, and saw Mark Johnson pick up a bald swordsman for producing *Rain Man*. This really must be my year; the following day I found out I'd won the Oscar pool at Weddington.

Larry did a major dogfuck on me for April Fools' Day. He called from Weddington, having been there for 31 hours straight, and said he had accidentally erased the time code on reel 5AB (which would have been a disaster). He let me twist in the wind a little before coming clean, the bastard.

3–10 APR 89

Bob and I met with Sydney Pollack, and hooked John Kao in by phone near the end. We discussed the book (or rather, the "project." Pollack explained that he read all of the material I sent him about the book but didn't have time to read the book itself) and came up with a basic structure. Pollack felt, and we agreed, that we shouldn't spend too much time on the ship, perhaps getting to the island at the end of the first act. He really liked the island part, the idea of trying to start from scratch, and felt we should get into that as quickly as possible. We all agreed the murder subplot should go, that the contact with the "beach people" should either be excised or handled in some other way, and that generally there was just some streamlining to do. I was happy to hear that he agreed the book was full of incident and cinematic ideas. He suggested pitching to Casey Silver in the near future. So he's in! Bob and I left his office shaking our heads. Where do we get off having this kind of luck?

Music mixing and recording was completed on the 5th, and was followed by foley and effects pre-dubs. On April 8th we started the final mix. This involves going from the SR-encoded analog multi-track to a Sony digital multi-track that will ultimately hold all of the conceivable mixes (stereo master, stereo minus-dialogue for foreign, TV stereo, mono, etc.). On the 8th we did reels 1AB and 2AB. On the 9th we did 3AB, 4AB, and up to the turnaround on 5AB. On the 10th we finished 5AB and 6A and that was it!! Now Larry has to go and prepare to transfer some of the various mixes to mag so they can be either shot to optical (the Dolby Stereo master) or delivered to Virgin (minus-dialogue mixes). I'm glad I don't have his job (although I've done my share of editorial assistant work, popping and syncing units, etc.).

11–16 APR 89

Now is as good a time as any to talk about the Cannes Film Festival. Miramax wanted to go, but wanted Virgin to split the cost. Virgin was willing to do that, but only if we got into the main competition. The film was screened for the main competition and rejected. Then the Director's Fortnight called and said they wanted us. Miramax said yes, but was having difficulty convincing Virgin that the Fortnight was worth the money. In the meantime (I am told), another American film dropped out of the main competition and suddenly *we* were offered a spot in the main competition. So then everybody was happy. Except me. I never thought going was a good idea. I'm convinced a huge backlash is around the corner, and where better to have a backlash than in front of the international press? I'm very flattered that we got in the main competition (as a rule, first-time directors have their films shown in the Fortnight), but I'm scared we'll get stomped. Spike Lee and Jim Jarmusch have films in competition this year, and I'm afraid we'll just get lost in the shuffle.

This week had a few levels of work going on at once. While Larry was doing the different audio mixes and spitting them onto mag, Walt and I timed the film at Telecine Tech for video mastering. On Friday we laid it down onto D2 (digital video) with the film interlocked to a DAT machine with the stereo print master on it (Larry gets a big kick out of carrying the print master in his shirt pocket. Normally a print master is five or six 2000-ft. reels of 35mm mag).

There is a big cast and crew screening at the Academy of Motion Picture Arts & Sciences on the 21st. The invitation list was huge (we couldn't make excuses to people anymore, since the theater seats 1100), and we're scurrying to get prints made for Cannes as well (three camera negative prints are required. One will be held for the Academy screening and shipped the following day). I'm wondering if there will be anyone left to pay to see the film when it's released (which will supposedly be in late August).

17–23 APR 89

Various and sundry shit, mostly getting the delivery materials together. Boy, it never seems to end, the amount of stuff required to finish up a movie. The night before the Academy screening I was at Weddington until 4:30 A.M. popping, syncing, and boxing all the various sound mixes that go to Virgin. It's good stuff to know how to do, actually, because you never know when you may need such knowledge (perhaps only to be able to tell when someone is doing it wrong).

The print for the Academy screening was too bright, and since the other two came from the same run and were already shipped to France, we can only assume those are bright as well. Walt worked out an arrangement with the projectionist whereby the output of the projection bulb was reduced enough to make the print appear to be at its proper density.

The screening was crazed. My mother drove cross-country with my stepfather, and I was looking around for my father and stepmother (who had flown in), but didn't see them. Bob told me at 8:10 that I had to get the thing rolling, and when I got to the podium they arrived, fortunately. My sister Susan and her husband Erik were there, as well as everyone everybody knew in Los Angeles, seemingly. I said a few words (specifically thanking the two Larrys, Blake and Estes), and got the hell out to the lobby, where I pretty much stayed throughout the screening (I occasionally stuck my head in to make sure everything was in focus). I bailed out just when the credits started, because I couldn't deal with the possibility of having to make introductory small talk with potentially hundreds of people. I talked to Pat Dollard later and he said it went very well. Peter Gallagher saw Jack Lemmon after the screening, and Lemmon apparently liked the film, which was great to hear (Peter had done *Long Day's Journey Into Night* with Lemmon on Broadway).

Jimmy gave me the best compliment an actor could give me: He said he felt like I cut his best performance together. That's a great thing to hear.

I think that's kind of the last of the big screenings. Actually, there are still a lot of little ones going on for critics and feature writers, which are only semi-nerve wracking. Clein, Feldman, White send me capsule responses by facsimile to Outlaw. The reception is good so far. Where and when will the backlash occur?

Future deal developments: Bob, John Kao, and I went over to Universal and hooked up with Sydney Pollack to pitch Casey Silver on *The Last Ship*. This is what happened: Bob, John, and I went over to Sydney's office first, basically agreed on what to say (and that Sydney should say it), then drove over to Casey's office (a three-minute drive). We walked into Casey's office and greeted Casey and Maura Manus. I've known Casey since he was at Tri-Star (he gave me my first movie-writing assignment. You know, the one I bought the Movado with), and I like him a lot. He's bright, speaks his mind, and when he makes a decision, he sticks with it, no excuses. I wasn't surprised when he became head of production at Universal. I'm setting this up because essentially I said seven words to Casey during the meeting, and two of them were his name. In between Sydney Pollack did a very passionate, eloquent pitch on why *The Last Ship* would be a great film

(I never said anything about *great*), and how I was the man (or boy, whatever applies) for the job. It was pretty masterful, I have to tell you. Casey rose, clapped his hands together, and said "Let's do it!" Gee whiz. Don't I have to show ID or something?

Elsewhere, Ron Yerxa and Albert Berger are on board with Barbara Maltby and Wildwood on *King of the Hill.* We're going to meet next week and talk details. Redford read the book, liked it, and is in the process of talking to Hotchner in person about obtaining rights.

24–30 APR 89

I was waiting for something bad to happen, and it did.

On Monday I received a facsimile of the *Rolling Stone* article, and as I read the first paragraph, I got sick to my stomach. I took it around and showed it to everyone in the office and tried to get them to tell me it wasn't as bad as I thought, but their "It's not that bad" responses sounded hollow, and their faces were drawn. The big problem was the first paragraph, wherein I was characterized as someone who sits around flippantly fielding phone calls, particularly those of Don Simpson and Jerry Bruckheimer, whom I called slime that barely pass for human (boy, I don't do anything halfway, that's for sure). The personal stuff about my life that embarrassed me to read, well, that's my life, I can deal with that. But immediately I knew that the Simpson/Bruckheimer thing was going to be a big problem (especially in view of the fact that I'd never met them), and I was right. Jim Berkus got a call from Don Simpson (who he knows well) that boiled down to Who Is Steven Soderbergh and Why Is He Saying All Those Terrible Things About Us? Jim tried valiantly to explain by pointing out that Lynn Hirschberg edited the "Hot" issue (Lynn having vivisected Simpson/Bruckheimer in *Esquire* some years ago in a piece that led me to my opinion of them). Simpson was still pretty pissed off. I spoke to Jim and said I wanted to make this thing right. I suggested that I write a letter of apology to be reprinted in an upcoming issue, and go apologize to them in person. Jim said that sounded like a good idea, and everything was arranged. I can't tell you how much this weighed on me for the period of time before I met with them (I imagined Sydney Pollack reading the quote and being deeply disappointed, to say nothing of my parents). Everyone I knew had problems with the article (although everyone liked the picture Bonnie Schiffman took), and I was frustrated because I had nobody to blame but myself. I didn't have the luxury of saying I was misquoted. It's my own fucking fault. I should've gone with my first instinct, which was not to do the interview. Ego took over, and I got what I deserved. Lesson learned.

So I went to see Don and Jerry (missing a screening of *Do the Right Thing* that Sam Kitt had invited me to), and got the "Oh, *you're* the one who said it" eye from the receptionist (well, at least she knew who I was). I said hi and they said hi, and I sat down and explained what happened, that I was very upset by the whole thing, and that it was my desire to write a formal apology letter. They said that sounded fine, that they didn't want to see me squirm or anything, they just wanted to know how I'd gotten this opinion, and I mentioned the *Esquire* piece, and Simpson smiled enigmatically and told me a pretty interesting story about how that piece came about. So we ended up talking for a while and they were exceedingly gracious. I felt a lot better when I left.

I talked to Terri Minsky. She seemed genuinely surprised and upset at what had happened. I want to believe that she really didn't think there would be any repercussions from what she wrote, but it's difficult. She said she's never spoken to a person that she's profiled after the piece has run, which I believe might be part of the overall problem. I ended up telling her that in the future she might want to think a little more about the effect on other people of what she writes. I really liked Terri, and I enjoyed the time we spent talking, but I don't feel I can have any further contact with her without seeming to condone what she wrote.

The day I saw the article I was so thrown that I forgot about a luncheon date I had with Ron Yerxa, Albert Berger, and Barbara Maltby. I met them the following day and insisted on paying for everyone's lunch. Business-wise, Barbara said Redford had spoken to Hotchner, everything was cool, and we could move forward. I then had to tell them that *The Last Ship* deal was set, and at minimum I was morally committed to doing that first (not to mention *Kafka*). They were kind of bummed, since they were thinking I was doing *King of the Hill* next. I explained that even though I met Barbara before I met Pollack, I didn't hear from her until after I'd essentially hooked onto *The Last Ship*. Barbara wasn't thrilled about going back to Redford and saying they were a few days late, which I understood.

1–9 MAY 89

Most of my time was spent coordinating the shooting of the conceptual footage for the trailer. We were using an endoscope lens, which
renders amazing footage but requires an enormous amount of light
(about 10,000 footcandles to get an image, which, when focused on a
small area, generates a lot of heat). I borrowed Bob's Video 8 to shoot
a test, and we were standing around at one point calculating an expo-
sure and I said "What's that smell?" We turned around to see Bob's
camera doing a Margaret Hamilton in *The Wizard of Oz.* So I had to
buy Bob another camera, and a couple of days later we shot the real
thing, and through the video monitor the stuff looked pretty spectacular. Six set-ups took all day, and I won't be able to see the footage until
after I get back from Cannes.

10–16 MAY 89 CANNES, FRANCE

Knowing that I will leave Los Angeles in the near future, I took the
Rambler to a mechanic and had the car to the airport pick me up
there. Jimmy and I flew over together, which was really great, because
it's a pretty long flight. Rod Steiger sat behind us. Boy, they really spoil
you in first class. I had serious white guilt.

I'll try to set down the high points, because it was pretty crazy.
First of all, it's a beautiful town, and arriving as the director of a film
in competition, one is very well treated.

There were, on Thursday, sporadic interviews and picture-taking
(I'll have to get over my problem of being photographed, because
there will be a lot of it). Things heated up Friday, because the *sex, lies*
press screening was that morning, and afterward there were a lot of
interviews lined up. Saturday there were more interviews and a press
conference, which was a lot tamer than I'd anticipated. I was expecting someone to stand up and shout "Your film is shit! Defend it!" and
I was prepared to argue. But it was actually enjoyable. That night was
our official screening, so we all got dressed up (me, Jimmy, Peter,
Laura, Nancy T., Mike Watts, Morgan, and Harvey Weinstein, among
many others) and went to the Palais. At the Palais, we were piled out
of our cars and then released to run a gauntlet of a thousand or so
photographers and fans while some Wagnerian bombast blared over
the loudspeaker system. Laura and I walked up together, and we were
pretty weirded out by the whole thing. It's disorienting to have a lot
of people you don't know yelling "Steven!! Look here!!" We watched

the film, which was actually an enjoyable experience, believe it or not. I'd never sat in a audience and watched the film end-to-end, and I found myself having a good time (Rob Lowe sat in front of me again. Is he following me?). One neat thing was that the laughter came in two waves; the first was from the French-speaking audience, because they could read the line before it was spoken, followed very closely by the English-speaking crowd. Some of the subtitle translations were funny, also. Peter saying "Roger" on the phone to Cynthia became "Five by five," which is a more international term for "okay," I think.

Afterward there was a standing ovation, and the cast and I stood and turned to acknowledge the response. It seemed like an eternity, and I looked over to Jean-Pierre Vincent, our French publicist, who was going to give us our cue to leave. Well, he made a motion with his hand that I thought meant "sit down," so I sat down. Then I looked over at him and he was motioning us to leave, so I got up, and there was some laughter. We went outside and weathered the crowd again, and went to the Majestyk bar to (hopefully) drink too much champagne. I met Spike Lee, who had seen the film and liked it, which surprised me (I thought he might write it off as a white-plight movie). We talked for a while, and he has a very wry, low-key sense of humor. I immediately understood how some of the things he's said in print might have sounded worse than they were because you couldn't see the slow smile on his face or hear the irony in his voice. I told him I was looking forward to seeing *Do the Right Thing* (and that the trailer had blown me away). He looked cool in a tux.

Laura and I were staying across the hall from each other, so we sat on my balcony and drank champagne until it started to get light out. It was a nice feeling. That was the last big screening, I'm convinced.

The next few days were nonstop interviews, with some time out to meet Jim Jarmusch, who was very nice. He introduced himself in the lobby of the Grand Hotel and invited me to the *Mystery Train* party. The next day I was on a panel of independent filmmakers with Spike Lee, Jarmusch, Wayne Wang, Charles Lane, and producer Edward Feldman *(Witness)*, moderated by the inimitable Sam Kitt. Jarmusch made some disparaging remarks about producers at one point that had everyone's ears burning. Jim also owns the negatives to all his films, which none of the rest of us could say.

So I left, exhausted and tired of talking about the fucking film. We survived, which is all I was hoping for. The reviews I've seen have been good, so everyone is happy. Overall, the festival wasn't as crazy as I had heard. People had told me "Oh, man, Cannes is crazy! Drugs everywhere, everybody's fucking everybody" and I didn't see any of that. Maybe I wasn't looking.

The rumor is we have a very good shot at winning the Camera d'Or, for best first film. I think that's nice, but I'm not counting on anything.

17–21 MAY 89 LOS ANGELES

After the Academy screening, Jeff Silver had delicately broached the subject of remixing the movie, primarily to smooth out 5AB a little more. I said I was open to it if I could talk the two Larrys into it (Blake to do it, Estes to pay for it). When I got back from Cannes, I was more definitively committed to remixing, and fortunately both Larrys said yes.

The footage we shot for the trailer is spectacular. I'll set up some time next week to cut it together. I'm very curious about Miramax's trailer, which I'm due to see next week.

Sunday I spoke with Mike Watts, who said it may be worthwhile for me to make a trip back to Cannes tomorrow. He had received a call from a festival representative asking if "someone" from *sex, lies* would be willing to return, which usually means there is a good chance of getting something. Mike said *Do the Right Thing* went down extremely well and would probably win the Palme d'Or. He felt we were pretty much a lock for the Camera d'Or, so I said I'd come back.

23 MAY 89 CANNES, FRANCE

I arrived and was immediately told that *sex, lies* had won the International Critics' Prize, which I was excited to hear. I went and received the award and then went to lunch with the Miramax folks. Rumors were flying about what was happening with the jury. Supposedly, they had been sequestered for much longer than normal, and absolutely no word was out on what was going to win what.

I went back to the hotel to lay down for thirty minutes or so before having to put on my tuxedo (which I hadn't cleaned since last week).

I don't remember walking up to the Palais. I remember being shown to my seat down on the third row or something, slightly to the right. I saw Spike Lee and Co. a few rows back, and I went over to talk to him. They all looked rather somber, and when I told him good luck

he said "We already heard." I asked him what he heard, and he
said he heard they weren't getting anything. I asked him if he was
sure, and he said yes. I went back to my seat and reported this to our
group (which consisted mostly of the Miramax contingent), and Harvey said that not long ago Festival President Gilles Jacob had told him
that we were going to have "a good night." We all shrugged and lights
came down and the presentation started.

Now, this is going to be kind of blurry, so bear with me. The
French emcee came on and said a lot of stuff in French (which was
only fair), and I had to get Demetra MacBride, one of the *Mystery
Train* producers, to translate (she was next to me). The Camera d'Or
was one of the first awards given, and it went to someone else. Everybody in our group looked at me. I shrugged, thinking to myself, well,
we got the Critics' Prize, that's pretty good. Some other awards were
given out, Yves Montand and Gregory Peck received tributes of some
sort, the *Mystery Train* group went up to receive the Best Artistic
Contribution award, Meryl Streep won Best Actress, and then somebody announced Jimmy Spader's name and I'm on my feet and walking up to the stage where Sally Field hands me a scroll and I give a
speech thanking everyone and saying that I knew Jimmy had a good
time in Cannes and would be overjoyed and then I walked off.

Standing in the wings I was just about to get my bearings back
and watch the rest of the show from backstage when some stage
assistant came up to me and asked who I was. I told him and he said
"Oh, I have to get you back to your seat." I thought, that's strange, none
of the other winners went back to their seats. So the guy leads me back
to my seat, and as I'm getting settled, Wim Wenders, the head of the
jury, is getting up to make the introductory speech about the winner
of the Palme d'Or. He starts talking about a film by a young filmmaker
and some other things and I'm trying to plug his comments into every
other film in competition, and while I'm still trying to narrow down
the possibilities he says *sex, lies, and videotape.* Suddenly it's like a
door opened and every sound in the world came out and I'm on my
feet again, and my heartbeat is throbbing in my surely red ears. This
time Jane Fonda hands me the Palme d'Or and I stand there for a
moment, waiting for the applause to stop and trying to figure out what
to say and trying not to fall apart. I looked out and said "Well, I guess
it's all downhill from here." I don't remember what I said after that,
and I don't think I want to know.

After the speech I had to come up to the lip of the stage to have
my picture taken by hundreds of photographers making that crickety

sound like in *The Right Stuff* and I'm just freaked and frozen and Jane Fonda is next to me asking "Are you all right?" and I was whisked offstage and put on live French television with two other directors, neither of whom looked particularly happy, and when the interview was over I got up to leave and a dozen laughing journalists pointed out to me that I had left the Palme d'Or underneath my seat.

Then they took me outside to shuttle me over to the press tent and these photographers were pushing in and screaming, it was like "ELVIS HAS LEFT THE BUILDING!" They got me into the press tent, where there was an impromptu press conference (I don't remember what I said. I know I told someone that I was stunned *Do the Right Thing* got shut out). Then I went to dinner with the Miramax folks and our publicity troops (who had busted their butts all through the festival. I'm pretty sure I thanked them from the podium), and we were all giddy at the craziness of it.

A sad thing happened then. We were coming out of the restaurant all happy and loud and we ran smack into Spike Lee and everyone from *Do the Right Thing.* They were very gracious in their congratulations, but they looked pretty bummed and I felt really bad for them. I felt like saying "I didn't ask for it, they just gave it to me, I didn't think we'd get this." But I didn't.

After unsuccessfully trying to get drunk (the adrenaline just kept sucking up the alcohol), I made a few calls to the States. The family was very excited. Seemed like a lot of people knew before I did, almost. They must have seen it on CNN or something.

Later, when everyone was falling asleep, Sam Kitt said "Well, if we had to lose to somebody, I'm glad it was you." I went up to bed and called a few more people. Nancy T. was in hysterics, Jimmy was as happy as I'd ever heard him, and Peter, who was in Paris shooting a movie, said everyone was crowded around a monitor and started yelling to him *sex, lies!* I called David Foil, who commiserated with me about the strangeness of it and kept saying "I just think it's great." He was right. I watched the sky get light and went through the congratulatory telegrams I'd received. Then I crashed.

24 MAY 89

I went out to this restaurant in the countryside called La Colombe d'Or with Alison Brantley, an executive from Miramax. We had a really nice lunch, and Mr. Francois Roux, the proprietor, did not allow us to pay, having seen me win the award on television last night (shit, I would have charged me double).

Around 11:00 or so Alison and I were having a last drink in the hotel bar and in walked Wim Wenders, Peter Handke, and Solveig Dommartin, the trio from *Wings of Desire* (Handke was also on the jury with Wenders this year). We drank champagne (I must be building up an immunity) and talked for a couple of hours. They were really great and it was the perfect way to end the whole Cannes experience. It was strange, though, to have Peter Handke say the film reminded him of Chekov, and the name that first popped into my head was Pavel, not Anton. We Americans are all the same.

Sometimes it just hits me all of a sudden, what happened, and I can't believe it.

26 MAY–4 JUN 89 LOS ANGELES

Decompression of a different type. I came back to see lots of articles about Cannes with my frozen face next to Jane Fonda. Doesn't seem real, somehow. I just can't compare *sex, lies* to other films that have won the Palme d'Or *(The Conversation, Taxi Driver, The Third Man, The Leopard, Wages of Fear)*, but at the same time, I'm not giving it back.

I met with Casey Silver, who basically wanted to reiterate his enthusiasm for *The Last Ship* and wish me well on the adaptation.

I met with Mark Johnson, Stuart Cornfeld, and Lem Dobbs, and we finalized a gentlemen's agreement to make *Kafka*. I liked Lem tremendously, and he was surprised and flattered that I had read his script way back when and remembered it. Stuart made me read another of Lem's scripts, *Edward Ford*, which was incredible. This guy is an intimidatingly good writer. He's a little older than me and just as skinny. So now I've gotten three "pet" projects set up with people I like and respect. I feel like I can leave town now.

5–11 JUN 89

Larry, Mark, and I screened *sex, lies* at the Burbank Studios to make notes about the new mix. We also invited Dale Strumpell, a sound mixer friend of ours, to give an extra opinion. It looks like pretty straightforward stuff, and Larry and I are especially pleased to have another shot without so much pressure on us. Dolby brought the gear back in and Larry and Cliff remixed some music. Virgin has decided to release a soundtrack, which is great.

I saw *Do the Right Thing* at Universal and loved it. I have to believe that no matter how bad he feels about Cannes, Spike knows in his heart he made a great film, and that is worth more than an award.

I reread *The Last Ship* and made some notes. I'm psyched about making it into a movie.

12–18 JUN 89

Met with Redford. It was fun, really. He's extremely smart and very candid, and I think we spent as much time talking about non-film-related issues as we did about business. We talked a lot about Hollywood, and what having a success in Hollywood can do to you if you're not careful. We talked about *King of the Hill* and he said he was very enthused about the project and I left thinking that the time had gone by very quickly. And for all you fans out there, I thought he looked even better in person than he does on-screen.

I also met with Pollack again to kind of shoot the bull and essentially make contact once more before I leave town.

Well, I cut my version of the trailer and I'm very happy with it, as is the Outlaw contingency. It's very unusual, but its mood perfectly emulates the mood of the film, I think, and one thing is for sure: It's not like any other trailer I've seen. Next week I'll see Miramax's and they'll see mine.

Larry was a mixing dude this week. He rented a device we weren't able to rent the first time to further clean up the dialogue, and it made a big difference. I came in at the end and we finaled on the 18th.

19–25 JUN 89

Well, Miramax hated my trailer, and I hated theirs. They hated mine because they felt it was "art-house death," meaning it was a little too esoteric, I suppose. Their trailer was everything I feared it would be, and more, with that song by Yello that was used so prominently in *The Secret of My Success* (I think it's called "Oh Yea" or something). However, the structure of their trailer was very good. I just hated the clip selection. So we got on the phone and a compromise was suggested—retain the structure of their trailer, use the footage I shot as a transitional device, and use some music from the film. Next week I'll get to see a new version.

There was a point some time ago when it became apparent that I would have a choice: I could ride herd over every little fucking detail of this movie's release or have some kind of life. I chose having a life, figuring I could deal with some minor things slipping through the cracks in order to be sane. So far I think I've made the right decision.

I wrote the liner notes for the soundtrack album. Initially I was going to try and be glib and funny, but after a few lame attempts I decided that for Cliff's sake I should just say what I felt. He's a really nice guy and he deserved a nice, no-bullshit liner note.

26 JUNE–8 JUL 89

Saw a version of the trailer that I liked. Miramax also came out to Los Angeles to show us some of the campaigns for artwork. There were fifteen or twenty different ideas, and I only liked one, which was a montage strip of two different pictures segmented and magnified to different degrees. Everyone else seemed to like it okay, so we decided to go with it. Harvey also talked me into doing the *Today* show (actually Harvey wanted me to do it, I said no, and Bob made an eloquent plea on Harvey's behalf).

Larry and I looked at a print with the new mix on it, and everything sounded okay. Now we have to make sure all the old optical soundtracks are destroyed, both here and abroad.

I met with Lem Dobbs and we went through *Kafka* line by line. Basically, I felt like we had to eliminate the girlfriend and family stuff and concentrate on the bureaucratic and thriller aspects of the script. We had a great time, and Lem seemed to pretty much agree with all of my suggestions. I hope my love for the material came through, because it is a great script. I tried to talk him into letting me do *Edward Ford* as well, but he wants to do it himself someday. I just have to make *Kafka* so great he'll beg me to do *Edward Ford*. Right.

9 JULY 89

Left Los Angeles by Rambler.

I had another interview this afternoon with Aljean Harmetz. Before we even sat down she said to me "You've changed." It's nice knowing the angle right from the get-go.

I got back to the apartment and prepared to leave while a documentary film crew shot my departure (these guys are doing a documentary about making it in the film business called *The Big Nipple*, based on Bertolucci's quote about Hollywood as a nurturing place to be. I am not making this up). It was really awkward because here I had Mark and Larry, two of my closest friends, trying to say good-bye with this camera crew and a journalist eyeballing us. And of course, I had to leave twice because the first time the shot didn't look right (nothing like staging reality. I should have refused), and the whole thing just . . . reminded me of why I was leaving Los Angeles, basically. I'll be driving at night to keep the car from running hot. Los Angeles to Charlottesville. Again, many are worried about the car making the trip. No faith, some people.

10–14 JUL 89 HEADING EAST

The routine went like this: Drive from 8 P.M. to 8 A.M., do phone interviews and check on various lab things, then crash until 6:30 P.M. or so.

The trip was actually quite pleasant. Driving long distances alone is very therapeutic. I stopped in Flagstaff, AZ; Gunnison, CO; Colby, KS; and Warrenton, MO. In Gunnison I stayed in a motel so cheap they didn't have phones, so I had to go down the street and tie up the pay phone at Kentucky Fried Chicken for half an hour.

I arrived in Charlottesville at 3 P.M. on Friday, and called the realtor who had written me when he read that I was returning to these parts (he actually tracked my father down and the letter was forwarded). We agreed to go look at rental houses tomorrow.

16 JUL 89 CHARLOTTESVILLE

Well, I found a house to rent. It was the first one I looked at, and of course I figured I couldn't just take the first thing I saw, so we spent several hours looking at houses that weren't as suitable before we came back to it.

Visited Bill Magee today, who was as kind and affable as always. I haven't decided yet whether I should let him read future screenplays.

17–26 JUL 89

Interviews. Boy, I was almost sorry I got a telephone (and a fax. I'm a sucker for faxes). The most interesting interview was with Katherine Dieckmann of the *Village Voice*, because she came down here and we actually got to spend a decent amount of time talking about a lot of things. The strange thing is that in an interview situation like that (and with Terri Minsky), I end up knowing as much about them as they do about me, either through questioning them or watching how they respond to my answers, and yet that never shows up anywhere. I don't get to give my view of what happened, or describe how they look (Aljean Harmetz characterized me as "a stork with wild blond ringlets"), or whether or not they're self-conscious or unhappy or overweight or whatever applies. I guess that's just part of the process, and I'll have to get used to it.

27 JUL 89 CHICAGO

A whirlwind trip to Chicago, where I did a solid day's worth of interviews. Gene Siskel asked me point-blank how many women I'd had sex with. I told him I'd never been asked that before, and he said he'd never asked anyone that before. I figured if he had the *cojones* to ask, then I'd answer, so I said "more than two, less than fifteen," which I thought could apply to almost anyone (Gene corrected my syntax, accurately stating that it should be "fewer" than fifteen, not "less"). My baggage didn't arrive until I was ready to fly to New York, so I got to give all my interviews in dirty clothing. Maybe it'll start a trend.

28–30 JUL 89 NEW YORK

The premiere is on August 1st (the Los Angeles premiere is on the 3rd), so I'm here doing more interviews. David Foil, who is moving to New York in two weeks, is flying up for the screening.

Spike Lee has been very vocal in his displeasure over the Cannes results, and all the interviewers ask for my opinion of his comments in order to get some static going. I tell them I don't have a problem with anything I've read on that subject, and this is why: I met Spike in Cannes and he said he liked my film, and if I'm a decent judge of character I don't think he disliked me. He has never said he thought *sex, lies* was shit, or that I was a jerk. He's very upset with the jury, Wenders in particular, and if I'd made *Do the Right Thing* and been shut out, I'd be pissed off as well (he said something pretty funny in *The Voice*, I think. He heard that Wenders commented that there were no heroes in *Do the Right Thing*, to which Spike replied "What's so heroic about a guy taping women?" He has a point).

3 1 JULY 89

In addition to interviews, I checked a test release print, which I deter-
mined to be unacceptable (way too red). I'll see another tomorrow.
The premiere is at the Ziegfeld, which I think is overkill, frankly, but
it was arranged before I could do anything about it.

1 AUG 89

Got up early to be interviewed by Bryant Gumbel on the "Today"
show. I reminded him on the air about his sordid past as a host on
"Games People Play," and he was quite surprised. He was a good
sport about it.

      Then the premiere. It started well, with lots of famous people
attending (I wondered how they felt about their "celebrity" status. I've
felt pretty unexceptional). The nightmare began when I realized that
I was seeing the SAME FUCKING LENS with the focus problem I had
seen used almost a year ago. I ended up going to the projection booth,
where I had this conversation with the projectionist:

ME *(A pained smile):* You seem to be having a problem keeping
    focus from edge to edge.

HIM: Yeah.

ME: When was the last time you had that lens collimated?

*Visions of the lens being chopped into bite-sized morsels danced in his
head.*

HIM: What?

ME: Collimated. Aligned. When was the last time this lens was
    aligned on an optical bench?

HIM: Well, it was put in here two years ago.

ME: Well, a projector vibrates quite a bit; this lens may just be mis-
    aligned. It's not just one piece of glass.

HIM: It's seven.

ME: Right, exactly my point.

HIM: We had the guy from Schneider come and look at it, and he couldn't find anything wrong.

ME: So you're just going to leave it that way?

He shrugged. It was a remote possibility that somehow the projection gate was manipulating the film plane, but I doubted it. I went downstairs and steamed, telling Miramax they shouldn't have to pay the full fee for renting the theater with that kind of presentation. You'd think at the goddam Ziegfeld you could get a focused image.

I rode to the party with David Foil and my stepbrother Geordy, who was here visiting a friend (who came along as well). The party was a fire marshal's nightmare, and I spent a lot of time talking to people I'd never met before, and no time talking to the people I'd invited.

After almost everyone went away, David Foil and I sat and shot the shit for a while. It was nice to just sit and appreciate the fact that my dreams of the past twelve years had become reality. It seemed insanely symmetrical that shooting started one year ago today. On the one hand, the last year and a half has gone by very quickly, but at the same time, I feel like three years' worth of events were compressed into that period. It's a strange sensation. I also think the reason a lot of suddenly successful people get screwed up is because they think they should feel better and be happier, and when they aren't, they think there must be something wrong with themselves, so they indulge in self-destructive behavior. What has happened to me is really great, but I don't feel any happier personally than I was eighteen months ago. I think it's a bad idea to tie your self-image to your perceived success in the film business. Could make one bitter.

2–3 AUG 89 LOS ANGELES

Still more interviews (and more to come. I've got three weeks of Europe coming up). I resisted the urge to give everyone completely different answers ("That's right, my mother didn't speak English, and Dad just rebuilt engines in the basement").

The film opens this Friday and then it will be out of my hands. There's nothing I can do for it anymore, save giving interviews.

At the Los Angeles premiere things went much more smoothly

(we had a semblance of focus on the screen), although Larry Estes and I got booted from the back of the theater by a very promotion-minded usher. The nerve.

The party afterward was nice, though once again I was besieged by well-wishers, which was fine; I just ended up not having time to talk to my friends (some said I was too gracious with strangers). I met John Waters, which was great. He's making *Cry Baby* for Universal, who he said has treated him very well. I think Universal is the place to be right now, as far as studios go. I think they understand that there is a marketplace for a lot of different kinds of films. Maybe I'm biased because I have two projects there.

The Los Angeles premiere was THE LAST BIG SCREENING. Now it's over, I'm convinced.

4 AUG 89

sex, lies, and videotape opened on seven screens in four theaters in New York and Los Angeles. Larry spent half the day lining up the audio for the five screens here (we are told Dolby recently aligned the Cinema Studio in New York). We had to pull Miramax's leg a little to do these alignments, but thank God we did. One system Larry checked had never been aligned after it was installed; all the pots were at the factory-default setting. Jesus, you can't take anything for granted.

Preliminary reports from New York indicate that both the screens at the Cinema Studio are selling out. Contrary to what some might expect, I do not want to go see the lines where the movie is playing, or watch the film with an audience. I want it to go off on its own.

I went bowling with Larry, Mark, and Cliff at the Pickwick Bowl in Burbank (with several other sound editors from Weddington). Afterward we went to a late movie and then Larry and I went back to his place in his Ugly Duckling rental car and I crashed on the couch.